How the f*ck would I know?

# How the f*ck would I know?

A memoir

Kate Rowe

Copyright © 2025 Kate Rowe

All Rights Reserved. No part of this book may be reproduced by any mechanical, photographic, or electronic processes, or in the form of a phonographic recording. Nor may be stored in a retrieval system, transmitted or otherwise be copied for public or private use other than for 'fair use' – as brief quotations embodied in articles and reviews, without prior written permission of the author.

ISBN: 978-1-7638925-2-1

ISBN: 978-1-7638925-3-8 (eBook)

A catalogue record for this book is available from the National Library of Australia

Cover concept by Angela McCarthy.
Calligraphy by Lindy Sardelic.
Proofreaders: Karen Crombie, Merren Smith, Mon Schafter.
Book design by Andrew Davies.
Project Management by Jane Turner.

Morning March. June 24th, 1978. Day of the First Mardi Gras, Sydney. Photo © Sallie Colechin.

International AIDS Memorial Candlelight Vigil, St Mary's Cathedral, 23 May 1994. Photo © C. Moore Hardy, courtesy Australian Queer Archives.

Disclaimer

Any opinions expressed in this work are exclusively those of the author and are not necessarily the views held or endorsed by others quoted throughout. All of the information, exercises and concepts contained within the publication are intended for general information only. The author does not take any responsibility for any choices that any individual or organization may make relating to this information in the business, personal, financial, familial or other areas of life. If any individual or organization does wish to implement the ideas discussed herein, it is recommended that they obtain their own independent advice specific to their circumstances.

*I acknowledge the Gadigal and Bidjigal people of the Eora Nation as the custodians of the land I live on and pay my respects to Elders, past, present and emerging.*

*I also pay my respects to those First Nations people who participated in the first Gay and Lesbian Mardi Gras Parade, Sydney, Australia 1978.*

*Dedicated to all my co-travellers who have faced your own demons and are also trudging the road to a happy destiny.*

## ACKNOWLEDGEMENTS

My family for loving me, even when I didn't think you did.

Jo Spangaro and Di Young for guiding me through my darkest years.

Jane Turner for staying with me and supporting me to make my dream real.

Donna Logue and the team from Generation Women for spurring me on to write this book.

Catherine, Jan and Maya for the lunches and encouragement.

Mon Schafter for accompanying me on runs and walks to mull it all over.

Lindy Sardelic for hooking me into Planet Ukulele and showing me that learning and playing can be fun, and grateful for your friendship.

All those I have connected and reconnected with, while putting this book together.

## CONTENTS

| | | |
|---|---|---|
| Acknowledgements | | 7 |
| Prologue | | 11 |
| Chapter One | Heritage | 13 |
| Chapter Two | They Know Not What They Do | 21 |
| Chapter Three | Dead Woman Walking | 39 |
| Chapter Four | Leaving the Mothership | 49 |
| Chapter Five | Confessions of a (Former) Drug Dealer | 57 |
| Chapter Six | Hitting Rock Bottom, Finding a Way Back | 63 |
| Chapter Seven | 1978 and All That | 87 |
| Chapter Eight | Just Another Statistic | 110 |
| Chapter Nine | Same Sex Marriage, Nineties Style | 132 |
| Chapter Ten | Paying it Forward, Almost | 139 |
| Chapter Eleven | My Best Mistakes | 144 |
| Chapter Twelve | A Love Letter to Cats | 150 |
| Chapter Thirteen | Deaths in the Family | 157 |
| Epilogue | | 189 |
| About The Author | | 201 |

Perhaps I had a wicked childhood.
Perhaps I had a miserable youth.
But somewhere in my wicked, miserable past
There must have been a moment of truth.

'Something Good'
From *The Sound Of Music*

Lyrics and Music by **Richard Rodgers**

Copyright © 1965 Williamson Music Company c/o Concord Music Publishing

Copyright renewed

All Rights Reserved  Used by Permission

*Reprinted by Permission of Hal Leonard LLC*

# Prologue

These lyrics from *The Sound of Music* totally sum up my musings and the reason I am writing this book, now that I am in my seventies. Getting older sucks, right? It's a seemingly endless round of visits to the doctors about changes, some trivial, some not. Of adjusting to physical limitations, of keeping moving in order to avoid turning into stone – not just yet. Of taking on challenges to keep the brain in tune. Of keeping an open mind. Of not settling for a dull routine of shopping, gossiping and lunching a lot. Of remembering what I went into a room for. Of forever putting things down and forgetting where I put them. Of waking up at two am and being unable to get back to sleep.

On the other hand, it's a chance to do what I like, to learn new things, to go to bed early if I feel like it, to spend time with the cat (or dog), to be politically engaged without marching in the streets, to spend time with friends old and new, to explore the world, the city I live in, and life outside of the retirement village.

Above all, it's a time to reflect on the last seventy-odd years. And on reflection, try to find those moments that might make sense of it all.

There wasn't any one event that showed me that moment

of truth people like to talk about. Rather, it has been a series of moments, seemingly unrelated (maybe not), with experiences and events that had profound effects and changed everything.

I call them a set of adventures. Some were hilarious, some pure magic (spiritual – not religious). Some were horrific, some traumatic, some dangerous, some downright stupid, and some were enriching. From the story of my forebears to my troubled immediate family, to child sexual abuse, to drug and alcohol addiction, to anorexia, the experience of rape, suicide attempts, recovery, and other good stuff.

Did I ever know what I really wanted to be when I grew up? Did I ever really grow up? Do we ever learn from our experiences? Do they make us better people?

How the fuck would I know?

So, I am writing this memoir in the hope that I might find out. Where my family is concerned, I want to stress that it is my experiences that I share with you here, and others I talk about are not always necessarily coming from my siblings' perspectives.

In any of the stories you read, you may discover similarities with your own experiences. Among other things, it's a reminder that we are not alone, even though sometimes it feels like we are in our darkest of dark times.

The chapters that follow are in chronological order, sort of, but not always. It won't matter if you miss one or two of them.

So jump in and join me on this yellow brick road and let's see where it takes us.

Kate Rowe

## CHAPTER ONE

# Heritage

**Where do we all come from, where do we all belong?**
As we get older, it seems that a desire to find out where we come from, and what our back story is needs to be crystalised. At least, that's what happened to me. My mother had four siblings; Ken, Kay, Jean and Wendy. All but Wendy have passed. Wendy is now 80, fading away from chronic depression in a mental hospital in the UK. Yes, we have mental illness in our family. It appears to be matrilineal, and I, for one, haven't escaped it.

Mum's mother was called Hazel, but we called her Gran. Mum's father was called Trevor and we called him Grandad. Dad's mother was called Helen, but we called her Nana. Dad's father left Nana when he was young, never to be seen again.

I have always had a desire to understand my complex family origins. My siblings, Helen, Peter, Simon and I would get snippets of information from Gran and Grandad, but there were parts of the story that didn't seem to add up. In particular, there seemed to be a veil of secrecy around Gran.

Here's a little bit of British history I'm throwing in for context. Though the British Empire still existed, many

Me on the right with extended family, 1964.

countries were handed back after WWII. This included India, which had been colonised. Firstly, it was under the rule of the East India Company which was an English company. It was formed to trade in the Indian Ocean region and seized control of large parts of India and Indonesia. There was an Indian rebellion, and in 1858 India came under British Parliamentary rule until 1947 when India gained its independence. Eventually, the British Raj faded into the sunset, but personal stories of those who lived there are still alive to this day, and form some of my heritage story.

Grandad was from Birmingham in England, born in 1899. He went to India and worked on the railways that the British Empire was building all over the country.

Gran is where the story gets interesting. She was half Dutch and half Indian. Her maiden name was Van Vink. We have managed to trace her ancestors to the Netherlands near Amsterdam as far back as 1650. One of the family became part of the Dutch East India Company. This ancestor was born in 1796 and became a missionary. We also believe one of our ancestors is buried in Amsterdam. Some of my family think that Gran may have been illegitimate.

We have no idea how Gran and Grandad met, nor where they were married, although there are records in a church in Calcutta that need exploring.

The family used to live in Calcutta in the winter and in Simla in the Himalayas in the summer. Simla was a favourite spot for those in the British Raj.

All of Gran's children went to boarding schools that were based on the British education system of the day. From what I have been told, it was not a pleasant experience.

Nana, 1930s.

Mum and Gran.

The British had to leave when Independence was declared in 1948. All of the family except for Ken went to Britain. Ken went to Australia and settled in Sydney.

My (late) sister Helen was born in 1949. A couple of years later, I was born in 1951. By this time Gran and Grandad were living in a council housing estate near Woking, close to where we lived until 1958. My two brothers arrived in 1953 and 1955. As kids we went to stay with our grandparents every week; girls one weekend, boys the next.

I have lovely memories of those times with Gran. Not so much my grandfather, as he had a foul temper and drank a lot. Gran used to wake us up with a cup of tea and a smile. She would cook dreadful curries, but made up for it with treats of Indian sweets to take the taste of the curry away.

She spoke with an Indian accent and had brown skin. I never questioned this – you don't as a kid, do you?

As time went on, I became aware that I had red hair and that mum and two of her siblings also had red hair and blue eyes. Aunty Kay had black hair, brown skin and brown eyes, though.

Sometimes when Mum put us to bed, we asked her if she spoke 'Indian', not knowing that the correct term was Hindi. I remember her saying that she spoke it more when she was younger and recited one to thirty in Hindi for us.

As we grew older, we asked more questions about what it was like growing up in India. She told us that the family had servants and Afghan dogs. To me, it seemed ideal, and with my propensity to live in a fantasy world, I would imagine wonderful days in the lower reaches of the Himalayas, just swanning around and not having to do much for myself. It wasn't that far from the truth really, but I remember my late uncle saying that the boarding schools were very strict and focussed on discipline.

In the '50s and '60s in Britain, there was a wave of migrants moving in from the West Indies, India and Africa. They were British Citizens because they had been colonised. Yet racism and prejudice were never too far under the surface.

It was just *not the thing* to have cross-cultural relationships in those days. So none of us were inclined to reveal our Indian past. I carried shame about it for quite some time, and never discussed it outside of the home.

What I found (and still find) interesting, was that when I travelled through Asia in the early seventies and arrived in Calcutta, I felt strangely at home. Not that I identify as Indian. I feel like that would be a stretch. Maybe because it was an ex-British Colony, or maybe there was a more spiritual connection going on. Whatever it was, these days I have no shame about my heritage. In fact, I feel like it's something to embrace. I have been told I look a bit Dutch, whatever that means. The British Empire was certainly a long period in Western history that left a great railway system but also left a lot of scars that are still being healed in former countries of the Empire (now the Commonwealth).

In retrospect, I can appreciate that never having felt a part of it, Mum and her family would have had a difficult time adjusting to life in post-war Britain, which was still recovering from the destruction. Going from a life of relative privilege to landing in a place with no roots and very little money or support of any kind, can't have been fun.

Nana's side of the family were also from Birmingham. Nana's real name was Helen Chambers. Her mother was a child musical performer, and both her parents were involved in old-time vaudeville. They eventually wound up managing a theatre and then owning a cinema back in the days when film was silent, and black and white.

With this background, I guess it's no surprise that Helen was also involved in entertainment. She had a beautiful alto voice and was a classically trained singer. In the '20s and '30s big swing bands were all the rage. Helen took a stage name with Raymond as her surname and made her debut at the Finsbury Park Empire in London. She described that performance as the most memorable of her career. She was also part of a group called The Rhythm Sisters. They were the British version of The Andrews Sisters. This was when our father and his brother were sent to a Catholic priory boarding school in Belgium.

Throughout the thirties until WWII broke out, Helen travelled the UK singing with dance bands like Ambrose, and the Jack Payne Orchestra, and performing with The Rhythm Sisters. She was a volunteer ambulance driver for those injured in bombing raids during the war, however, she was also in demand as a singer and performer working at the BBC. As the 'wireless' was the main form of entertainment, Helen switched to radio. In the post-war period, television was starting to make an impact, so it was no surprise to find that Helen was also involved in the early days of TV.

In 1947, she went off to the US hoping to further her career. She was there until 1954 having failed to get the necessary Green Card she needed to be able to work there. Post-war Britain had changed, along with the popular music of the day. That's when Helen decided to retire. It was a decision, she told me, that she never regretted.

She returned to the UK and lived near us in Putney in London. It was our duty to visit her on Saturdays and do her laundry. It was Helen and I one week and Peter and Simon the next. We always wondered why she had an American accent, but now we know. Even as she became older and smoked a lot, her voice was still beautiful.

I managed to spend some time with her on my first visit back to the UK in 1989. Strangely, she died a week after that visit, and I was able to attend her funeral. She was never one to be emotional or physically demonstrative, but she did share some family secrets with me. I'm not sharing them in this book (or anywhere else for that matter) because, as far as I'm concerned, they need to stay that way.

What I find amazing is that Nana still has a fan club, and there are several old films of her performing solo and with The Rhythm Sisters that can be found on YouTube.

So there was a real heritage in the form of the cultural influences that were passed on to the next generation in my family. This is not so unusual in the current iteration of the planet. In fact, it has become a by-product in the era of globalisation. Similarly, the nineteenth and twentieth centuries were shaped by events of their time, just as it is in the twenty-first century.

*Plus ça change!*

## CHAPTER TWO
# They Know Not What They Do

Trigger warning.
This chapter contains details of childhood sexual abuse.

The heading of this chapter is such a bland phrase. Behind it was a child who lost her innocence, learned to lie, keep secrets, and never knew how to have a healthy adult relationship when she grew up. Her pattern of dysfunction was set early on in the piece, and it changed the course of her life in so many ways. That child was me.

I was known then as Katie by my family. Like so many kids, our beginnings in life were not all great. When I was five and Helen my sister was six, we were packed off to a Catholic school as boarders. It was a very traumatic experience, being dropped off at the big wooden gates and seeing my parents walk away. I experienced such intense separation anxiety that I cried for three days and the nuns couldn't console me. The nuns were very strict, and I recall slaps of a steel ruler on the back of my legs and hands. We were taken out of the convent after two terms, it seems because my parents didn't like the kind of corporal

Age 5.

punishment which was so common then.

That trauma of being left by my parents, which made me feel totally rejected, was the building block of what became a pattern in my relationships. The pattern was to leave before they did, to spare myself the pain, or I would sabotage my relationships in some other way. Inevitably my partner would leave, and I would feel rejected. It was such a tragic loop to be stuck in.

Meanwhile, my sister and I were very often left to look after ourselves and our younger brothers at home. I didn't mind that so much, but I actually hated living in a London Council housing estate. I relished being in nature and had a great curiosity around life in general. I also had a creative imagination.

Our primary school was on the estate. We would get dropped off before school and stay for after school care. I had friends at my Comprehensive High School and in my first year I was doing OK. Just like any other girl.

We were left to our own devices a lot of the time, but in retrospect I can see that we really needed supervision. I remember many instances of being molested when travelling on buses or on the Tube and on Putney Heath between the ages of 8 and 11. And of course, I was too frightened to tell my parents. So this pattern of sexual molestation that played a significant part in my life started very early.

I started to do a Saturday paper round in the private housing area next to our council estate, along with my sister Helen. Helen met up with a gardener working there and started to babysit for him on Saturday mornings. She was given ten shillings for her trouble. She didn't last long,

## Chapter Two

though. I do wonder if what happened to me, happened to her. That would explain her leaving so abruptly, and never saying anything about why she left. It was only about six weeks before she asked me if I wanted to take it over. Of course, I said yes, because I wanted to buy one of the new transistor radios that were a whopping five pounds at the time. So the babysitting was going to be great pocket money for me.

Before I started, I went around to meet John and baby Jessie (not their real names). Jessie was only eighteen months old at the time. John's wife had left him for his best friend, and he needed a sitter to look after Jessie who was only a toddler. I innocently took the job on. I was eleven years old and I had no idea what I was letting myself in for.

At first, it was all good. I loved looking after Jessie and keeping her entertained, teaching her all those things that toddlers need to learn, including how to read. She was like a sister to me really. I often stayed for lunch.

Another reason I liked going there was because it got me out of my own home which I was increasingly not liking. Among other things, there were a lot of arguments going on at home, especially around money. Both parents needed to work, so all four of us were 'latchkey kids'. That, as well as spending Saturday mornings looking after Jessie, gave me a space where I didn't have to deal with all of the ongoing conflict in my home. This arrangement went on for a few months. John and Jessie were invited to come around and meet my parents, and they kind of became part of the family really. At one time I even went with John and Jessie to visit his family in Birmingham. All was well. Then it changed. I remember after a meal once when Jessie was in bed, John

With Jessie, 1964.

With Jessie, meeting after 56 years, 2022.

## Chapter Two

started to touch my body. He told me he was going to teach me how to kiss, and for a few weeks that is what we did. By then I was twelve and teenage hormones had begun to appear. I was both scared and excited at the same time. I had no idea anything was wrong with what was going on, and I just went along with it.

I didn't know I was being groomed. Then one day he started moving his hands towards my groin while kissing me. He told me that this is what grownups do. Whilst it never involved penetration, I had my first orgasm at 12. This took things to a new level. Then he started saying that I mustn't tell anyone, and to keep it a secret, which I did.

Then I started to go to his place after school and stay until about 9 pm. I told my parents I was at John's looking after Jessie, and they were fine with it. They didn't seem to worry. I always made sure I was back home at the promised time, and they never asked me why I was there for so long. The pattern was that I would bathe Jessie and put her to bed, and when she was asleep, the sex would happen. I need to own the fact that my sexual awakening was a huge rush, and I spent as much time in anticipation of this happening as I could. I blamed myself for a long time about this, but was told in therapy that it was not my fault as it was part of the process of being groomed.

What I didn't like was keeping a secret and lying to my parents. I started to change from being an open, playful child to being a quiet, insular girl. At school I would fall asleep, and my good grades started to fall. I was very good at sport and loved it, though. I had also been learning the piano since I was seven, but that went out the window. I seemed to go into a dark place where no one could touch me. I was deeply depressed without knowing it. My discipline and interest around homework slipped away. I also stopped seeing my friends, instead spending all of my spare time with John and Jessie. It was like I had another home where I was playing the part of a wife and mother. There were several times when John told me that he loved me, and wanted to marry me when I was sixteen.

I had to choose a path in my third year at school. The options were to do my GCE's or take a vocational route. I simply had no idea what I wanted to do, and my confidence and self-esteem seemed to have disappeared by that time. I was locked in a dark space, and I had no support or anyone to talk to about my options. Back then the teachers were not educated in picking up signs of child abuse.

As my school was a comprehensive (which means that it wasn't full of high achievers who had to compete to get a place like they do in the selective high schools) it catered for varying streams of vocational training. I went to a lunch at the pre-catering department and decided I wanted to be a cook. I could cook pretty well already, but for me, it was a way of not having to deal with my insecurities around academia, which I had all but given up on by that stage.

All the time the sexual encounters were going on, my odd behaviour was starting to show. I started the two-year pre-catering course, but I was being quite troublesome and asked my parents to take me out. Fortunately I got into a prestigious catering college in London. This took up more of my time, but I was still able to find time to see John and Jessie.

Then one day my father came home with the news that he had been offered a job in Manchester and that we were all going to move up there in about three months. So at seventeen, the sexual relationship I had with John ceased.

After a five year 'relationship' I was out on my own and feeling terribly lost. The most obvious way I acted that out at that time was by having casual sex. I had come to believe that the only way you could have a friendship with a man was to have sex. I trusted no one. I didn't want to be in Manchester where I had ended up and had to start a new life.

Deeply unhappy, my self-destructive drive took over for the next twelve years. I got into drugs and alcohol with a special place in my heart for the drug scene. Basically, I had almost zero insight into what I had become. I had no ability to say no to sex, nor to alcohol or drugs. All I knew was that I didn't want to be 'in reality', and the only time I felt confident or happy was when I was 'out of it'.

The worst thing for me was that I totally, and I mean *totally*, repressed and suppressed that five years of abuse I experienced. I never talked about it to anyone, and never even thought about it if I'm honest. I feel like I had completely disassociated from who I was.

It wasn't until I was in my late twenties that I had an inkling of something strange and dark inside me. I had returned to Australia after three years back in the UK. I was exploring politics and had attended a Marxist Summer School in Sydney. There was one class where some of the men were talking about their love for children within a Marxist paradigm, which at the time I thought was abhorrent. I didn't understand the discourse, but what happened next was deeply disturbing. I suddenly felt this enormous emotional pain hit me right at my core. I went into a spare room and found myself in a foetal position, wailing and crying for the pain to go away. This outpouring of emotion went on for about twenty minutes and finally subsided. I told no one. In fact this is the first time I have mentioned it. Why? Because I was embarrassed. I felt that there was something terribly wrong with me and that I would be laughed at if I told anyone about it. I had no idea what the visceral experience I went through was about. But knowing what I know now, it's pretty clear that it was the first iteration of my trauma rising to the surface and was an episode of catatonia.

In that same year, I was coming to terms with my sexuality and started having affairs – many of them. I fielded a few comments from my lovers about the fact that when we made love I scared them with a dark aura. None of this made any sense to me at all at the time. I was incapable of having long term relationships, because I thought that once my partners got to know me, they would see how sick I was. So rather than having to go through the process of being rejected I would finish the affair, using the fact that I was moving around as an excuse to end the relationship.

I could see that there was something wrong with me. I just couldn't understand (let alone verbalise) what it was. I simply didn't understand how scared I was.

Then in 1987, I was violently raped in my own home. By this time I had been clean and sober for a number of years, and I was in a recovery program. Once I started what was to be my many years of therapy, this particular episode of sexual abuse finally surfaced. If I thought the rape itself was traumatic, opening up about my childhood abuse just tripled the intensity. And basically, I had a breakdown.

## Chapter Two

At the time, I was in what felt like was going to be a permanent relationship. I loved this woman, but I was blind to my co-dependency, and that same fear of 'if they knew who I really was, they'd leave me', was playing out in the back of my mind. In any case, the relationship was in trouble, and going into intense therapy on top of the impact of the rape just made matters worse. In the end, the relationship broke down about a year after the rape. Looking back on it now, I can see that it was just too much for anyone to have to deal with a person who had fallen to pieces to the point that they were not coping with anything. So I actually had three major traumas to deal with at that point.

I embarked on an eight-year long and dark emotional journey of healing. The bottom line was that no matter how tough my circumstances got, I resisted picking up a drink or a drug, and I didn't even take any medication.

I joined an incest survivors group that went for twelve weeks. Through that, I started to make sense of what had happened and to call it for what it was. Through all sorts of therapeutic tools, like art, writing, sharing, expressing anger safely, and going through the sheer emotional pain involved in healing, my experience started to make sense and shine a light on the reasons for my past and current destructive behaviour. I started to see how this experience had permeated my whole way of being in the world. To some degree it still affects me. I had no concept of boundaries. This lack of boundaries was an inherent part of all of my affairs and relationships. The main issue was that because I didn't have any boundaries of my own, I would often crash through other people's boundaries, and that would create all manner of emotional and mental problems for both of us.

This process was on top of doing the same sort of work about the rape itself. It was a very long eight years of deep pain, anger and resentment around how my life had been changed and would never be the same. As each new revelation and understanding came about, there was a form of acceptance I found that enabled me to see that while I couldn't change what had happened, I could change how I dealt with its legacy in my current life.

I was diagnosed with PTSD and over time have mainly learned how to manage it, yet at times it can be triggered by stress and feeling trapped. It can take days to come out of that awful space.

In 1989 I received a modest amount of compensation for the rape, and I knew that I wanted to go back to the UK to visit my family for the first time in twelve years. So I booked my flights and paid for them with some of the money I had been awarded.

With the abuse now out in the open, I decided that I would like to meet John and tell him how my experiences with him had changed my life. I wrote a letter to him to say I was visiting London and asked if he would like to meet me, not saying anything about why. To my surprise, he said that he would love to. I sought counsel on how to deal with the situation. Some people said I should leave it alone, and that I was crazy to meet up with an abuser. Others thought I was brave. I felt neither of these things. It just felt like the door had been opened, and I needed to try to resolve some of the things that continued to bother me as part of my healing process. Part of that entailed having some faith in myself, and trusting that I would be OK, no matter how painful it was.

## Chapter Two

I duly went ahead with the meeting. He picked me up at Fulham Broadway Tube station and we went to a pub. By now he had remarried, but he came alone. I got an inkling of how much he hadn't changed when I got in the car. He immediately went to kiss me on the lips. I asked him to stop, which he did. It took all of my emotional strength not to react by screaming at that point.

We had lunch and got talking about the five years when he was taking advantage of me. I mustered all my courage and told him (not in an angry way) that I knew now that what took place was sexual abuse. I went on to say that it had left me feeling disturbed and dysfunctional, and that I still suffered in that way as an adult.

The positive thing was that he didn't deny it. But he said he loved me then and still loved me to that day. The one statement he made that I am still both hurt and bewildered by, is that he told me that my mother knew what was going on (how, I don't know), and that she was colluding with him because she thought it was a good education for me. Was this John manipulating me and trying to justify his actions while not taking responsibility for what he had done, or was he telling the truth? I never found out, and probably never will. I choose to think it was a case of a sick perpetrator manipulating me. It just hurts too much to think that my mother, whose relationship with me was sickly symbiotic and who had her own mental issues, would say that having to endure years of sexual abuse was a good education.

I just have to live with that uncertainty, I guess.

At the end of our private conversation, John said he was sorry that it happened, and that if it was any help, he had become impotent and maybe that was karma.

We then went back to his home and I met his wife. We spent a couple of hours reminiscing about that time all those years ago when I was Jessie's babysitter, and he brought out photos of me and Jessie. He told me that Jessie had become a troubled child, and how she'd gotten into all sorts of trouble as an adult. But there was no mention of the abuse. It was clear to me then that his wife had no idea what he had done.

I went away feeling like something had shifted, and that a bit of healing and lightness had filtered in. I thought that I could leave it all behind me. In some way there was a degree of acceptance of the damage that was done. And yes, sadness that it had happened. But I honestly thought that I could move forward, and the damage would go away.

Over the next few years, as the issue of redress for child sexual abuse was becoming more available via the justice system, I thought about going down that avenue. For me, it would have meant going back to stay in the UK. I'd kept the idea that harming others in order to aid my own healing was best avoided in the forefront of my mind. And, given that I hadn't told Jessie about what had gone on, I decided not to go down that path. I know that many would have made a different decision, but for me, going on that journey just didn't feel right. For the most part, I put that decision down to the effect of the ongoing trauma I was still experiencing from the rape. That's how deep and profound the effect of childhood abuse is in a person's life.

I also chose not to have any contact with John again. However, in 2019 I was back in the UK and I had set up a cat-sitting arrangement in Putney, the suburb I grew up in and where the abuse took place. By this time I wondered if he was still alive, and the idea to go back to the scene of the crime was floating around in my head. Most of the time, I dismissed that thought. I think my motivation was to be able to say that whilst I would never forget what had happened and the damage it had done, I forgave him, and in the process, I would be forgiving myself.

Then one day I was walking up Putney Hill and passed the street he lived in. I made a spontaneous decision to go and see if I could find his flat. I did, and knocked on the door thinking that he probably wasn't going to be alive anymore.

His wife answered the door but I didn't recognise her. She was now in her late eighties. I asked if John still lived there. She called out to him and he came to the door. It was clearly a surprise to them both, but I was invited in for a cup of tea and a chat.

Once again we talked about old times and more photos were brought out and stories were told. He told me that they had both had serious illnesses they were dealing with, but that they were coping. All I saw this time was the image of a frail old man that I found almost impossible to reconcile with my memory of the man who had abused me for years.

I then brought up a discussion we had when I visited them in 1989, and I was gutted by his response. He said that he didn't remember any conversation. I realised very quickly that what happened was still a total secret and that he had not told his wife yet. So he was sitting there blatantly denying the truth. Somehow, I managed to keep my emotions in check and not let on how painful it was for me. I looked at his wife who had her head down whilst I was talking, and my sense was that she had worked it out. I made the decision to just let go of it because I didn't want to damage others in my quest for peace. With that, I gave them both a hug and went on my way, thinking that it would be the last time I saw him. That turned out to be the case.

I went back to the UK in 2022. In the interim, I had told both of my brothers about John and the abuse. They were both shocked. This time I decided that maybe I could meet Jessie, but I had no idea where she was, or if she would even remember me.

This is where social media came into its own for me. I searched her name on Facebook, and even though 58 years had passed, I recognised her, and she recognised me from the photo I added to the message I sent her.

She said, "Of course I remember you, and of course I want to see you again." And so we arranged a time to catch up. She told me that both John and his wife had died, in 2020 and 2021.

I had previously sought counselling that included whether I should tell Jessie about her father and the abuse I suffered at his hands. I didn't want to harm her at all, and part of me was saying no, while another part was telling me to keep an open mind.

I got to the theatre in the West End where we had arranged to meet, and I recognised her immediately. We screamed and hugged, and screamed and cried, and hugged again. We walked to a nearby park where we sat for nearly three hours just talking and sharing our stories.

Listening to how her life had been since she was five was hard. It had been very tough for her, and she'd had some awful things happen to her. She had a very strained

## Chapter Two

relationship with her father, and acted out a lot of her issues in ways that did her no good.

Then it was my turn. I told her about my move to Australia, my drug and alcohol problems, and that I had been clean and sober (at that time) for 45 years. I also told her that I was a lesbian, and that my track record with relationships was pretty poor.

As we were sharing our stories, it felt like she had no idea about me and John. So he had successfully kept it a secret from her. Because of that, I wasn't planning to bring it up.

Then she said, "So what was your relationship like with John?" The last thing I was expecting was a direct question like that. I am an honest person, and instead of saying anything, I just started crying. My emotional response to that question was so painful that I couldn't hide it. So I told her. She was shocked, and asked me many questions. I did my best to answer them. Then she told me that she had been pack raped as a teenager, so she knew what abuse was. Then she said that what John did wasn't as bad as what had happened to her. I was so upset inside, my stomach just churned and I kept crying. In that moment I couldn't put into words what the kind of abuse I experienced did to a young girl. At the same time, I didn't want to judge her for not understanding what it was like for me to be living with the legacy of the awful things that had happened to me.

We both had to leave, and I told her that I was going to Germany, but that I was coming back to the UK for another week, and wanted to meet up with her again before going back to Australia. It wasn't just about getting a bit more closure for us both. It was also because I was concerned about her.

It was late by the time I got back to the place I was cat-sitting at in Wallingford, Oxfordshire, and I was physically and emotionally exhausted. I went to bed, and as I always do, I turned my phone off. I didn't turn it on again until later the next morning. That was when I noticed that she had called me three times through the night with pleas for me to contact her, saying that it had been hard to hear what I had said, but that she was still OK with me, and hoped that I was OK with her. The message finished with her saying that she wanted to talk to me.

Our only contact had been via Facebook Messenger. I immediately sent through a message with my apologies for not responding sooner, and with dates that I could come back up to London to meet up with her. Then a message came up saying that her page was unavailable. I asked someone who was a bit more savvy than me when it came to social media about what was going on. She told me that I had been blocked. It seemed like Jessie hadn't read my last message and maybe went away thinking I had rejected her. I hated thinking that could be the case.

I went into a total spin. I felt disgusting and was sure that I had harmed her by making a most hideous mistake. I was scared that she might harm herself or have a breakdown of some kind, and that it was all my fault.

I returned to Australia a week later and was booked to go to a women's recovery retreat. I spent most of the weekend curled up in a state of despair and self-hatred. I now blamed myself for harming Jessie, and thought that maybe I should have kept the abuse of me by her father a secret.

I went into therapy for about six months as I knew I needed a lot of help to come to terms with what I had done

## Chapter Two

and accept that I couldn't change what had happened, and needed to let it go. What made it really hard for me to do that was that I had absolutely no control over the situation because Jessie had blocked me, and I had no phone number, home address, or email address to get back in touch with her.

At the end of the six months of therapy, I wrote a short note with the help of my therapist that one of my brothers agreed to paste on her Facebook page, even though he told me that she had not been on Facebook for over two years.

It is now 2025 as I'm writing this book, and I still haven't had any contact with Jessie. Either I am still blocked, or she has left Facebook and Instagram. It took me about a year to let go and accept that I am powerless when it comes to wanting to clear the air with Jessie, and that I may never be able to make amends or find out how she is going.

I know that the ball is in her court and that she can contact me via Facebook if she ever wants to. I will remain open and willing to catch up with her should the opportunity arise. It is no longer up to me. Sometimes the memories of this journey come to the fore and I feel the emotional pain again, and again I ask the universe for forgiveness. Sometimes in life, letting go is the hardest thing to do.

## CHAPTER THREE
# Dead Woman Walking

**Trigger warning.
This chapter contains details of anorexia.**

The title of this chapter sounds pretty harsh, doesn't it? But that is exactly what I turned into for two years when I was 18.

Back in 1969, eating disorders were virtually unknown and rarely reported. There was only one medical text that described anorexia at the time. So how was it that I went down this potentially fatal path?

Early on in my teenage years, I was quite focused on body image and had a distorted perspective of what I looked like. But I wasn't the only one. Today it's called body dysphoria. My sense is that younger women who are going through puberty might balk at the sudden changes their body goes through and be triggered into a pattern of disordered eating. What I did was start cutting out my lunch. Using 'diet' meals in a biscuit was a popular way to keep the weight off back then. I did lose weight, but I kept that fact as a secret from everyone. And my parents and teachers didn't seem to notice.

This was the era of Twiggy, after all. For younger readers,

Age 18.

Twiggy was a hugely successful international supermodel from London. She was all of 20 years old, and weighed in at 41 kg. In fact, she was a tiny woman who was only 167 cm tall.

It was a time when young teenagers wanted to look like Twiggy, and magazines directed at teenagers were full of beautiful, young, skinny women just like her. So it's no great surprise that suddenly everyone wanted to be extremely thin.

I was already slim at 17 when I first became aware of Twiggy. I was certainly in no doubt about what the look at the time was supposed to be, though, that's for sure.

Then in 1968, I had a boyfriend who commented that I had a fat belly and looked pregnant. I don't know how or why those words went through me like a knife, but this was the start of my hidden self-hatred being given a voice (so to speak). And like so many others, I started to compare myself with Twiggy.

I was living at home at the time. My sister who I shared a bedroom with, had joined the Royal Air Force and wasn't home much. The obsession with how I looked didn't take long to take hold. I became quite self-centred and started to diet again. I would eat with the family but say that I wasn't hungry and leave half of what was on my plate uneaten. I again kept my dieting a secret from everyone, and started checking my weight every day. It was not like I had a lot to lose, but I wanted to be like Twiggy so that I would be liked again.

My parents were preoccupied with their own lives and didn't pay much attention to me. My mother was studying for a PhD. In fact, she was driven by it, and my father spent all of his time supporting her.

Then the strategies I was using to restrict the calories I was taking into my body got serious. I would cook for the family on Sunday and keep them all out of the kitchen which I made gorgeous meals. And then I wouldn't eat anything myself, and keep myself busy doing all of the dishes. I seemed to be shutting down and shutting off from my surroundings as the weight started to disappear, and yet, I saw myself as fat. This is how dysmorphia works. My disassociation with my body had taken a dangerous turn, and I really had turned into a dead woman walking!

I kept this regime up for months, eating less and less food each day. What little I did eat became a ritual. My weight kept going down and down. Finally my parents took notice as it was obvious I was way too thin and that something was wrong.

In tandem with this happening I went into a deep depression and stopped communicating except for monosyllabic responses to the questions my parents were asking me. Depression is talked about as a black dog. I am not sure if that fits my experience of it. It was more a case of my having fallen into an abyss of nothingness. It was a world where all was dark, a world where I thought no one could touch me, and where I felt nothing. The less I ate, the deeper I went. I started to keep a diary. It was pretty grim reading because I was full of dark thoughts, suicidal ideation and self-hatred.

There were two turning points that started to shift my warped and self-destructive inclinations. The first one happened when I went into a shop to buy a bikini. Why, I don't know. I tried it on in the communal changing room.

This resulted in everyone staring at me. I had no idea why they were staring at me, but it would have been impossible for me not to notice that they were.

The second time was at home when I put on the bikini I had bought to show my family. My elder brother actually broke down in front of me and cried loudly as he begged me to STOP. For my part, I couldn't get my head around why he would say something like, "Why are you doing this, please stop!" The fact that I couldn't fathom what his problem was came down to the total disassociation I had achieved in relation to my body, and the high degree of dysmorphia that had developed.

It was at this point that my mother took me to our local doctor and pleaded for help. That resulted in a referral to a psychiatrist. I went into the consulting room with my mother to find a small group of students in attendance. The psychiatrist undertook a medical examination of me, and was pointing out how low my heart rate was, how cold my skin was, and my extreme thinness, noting that these are the signs of anorexia. The result of the session was that I was put on anti-depressants and sent home with a follow-up appointment scheduled in.

The result of this was that nothing changed.

During the next visit, again with my mother, the psychiatrist tried to engage with me, but I was in a veritable 'closed cell', and refused to speak. He then sent me out of the room to talk to my mother alone. I was then called back in and he told me, without providing any real context, that I would never gain my mother's acceptance, and that what I was doing in terms of losing weight wasn't going to change that. For whatever reason, this struck a deep chord in me.

He then weighed me and found that I had gone down to 39 kg. He was quite stern with me at that point, and warned me that if I dropped to 38 kg he would have to admit me to the mental hospital. This didn't really scare me because I thought it was just another downward step on the ladder to the end.

The following two or three weeks were just the worst. In the end, I was only eating one scone a day and drinking numerous cups of coffee. I became so weak and depressed that I couldn't get out of bed, and then, when I thought things couldn't get any worse, I came to the point where I was unable to eat anything.

One day, when I was alone in the house, I completely broke down and wanted to take any pills I could find. Inside I was screaming for help. It was the same voice that my shattered soul told me to reach out for someone or something to help me. I only knew of Lifeline at the time, so I called them.

That call was the start of a very slow healing process. Minuscule shafts of light started to penetrate the dark, personal prison cell that my life had become. I started to get a sense of hope that I could get out of this quagmire of darkness that I had taken myself to.

The words that my psychiatrist had said about my mother felt like some vindication of the years and years of attempting to gain acceptance from her. As it turned out, the same thing played out with my father later in life as well.

Coming back from the brink of death with a mental illness such as anorexia is a difficult and painful journey for all of those around us.

It was a really scary place for me as well, because breaking the habit of being skeletal and starting to eat again meant putting on weight, and that meant facing many of my fears. It was these fears that took me down the path of destruction in the first place. These fears had been with me for all of my short life. They were manifested in the fear of leaving childhood and becoming a woman. There was also fear of rejection that resulted in my desperately seeking approval, especially from my mother. As well as fear of abandonment, and fear of failure. There were so many fears, some of them unknown and not understood. All of these fears and the way they showed up in my life were in some ways self-fulfilling.

Becoming anorexic was, I thought, the way I could control my world. I believed that no one would be able to touch me, and that I could literally 'disappear'.

Did I face up to those fears? Not really. However I did gradually come out of my shell. The main catalyst for that was that I had applied and was accepted for a migrant passage scheme, targeting families and single women, to travel to Australia. I then joined a growing number of people who were colloquially called Ten Pound Poms.

To a then-twenty-year-old woman like me it was an adventure that gave me something to look forward to. This actually brought me out of the darkness I had cocooned myself in. I thought I could leave everything behind and start a new life without all of my baggage. The problem I was to discover, of course, was that I WAS the baggage!

Reflecting on it fifty or so years on, one of the consequences of being anorexic included not having a menstrual cycle for seven years. This is because our bodies shut down when we are underweight, and it took me that long to get back to a weight that would switch me back on again. During that

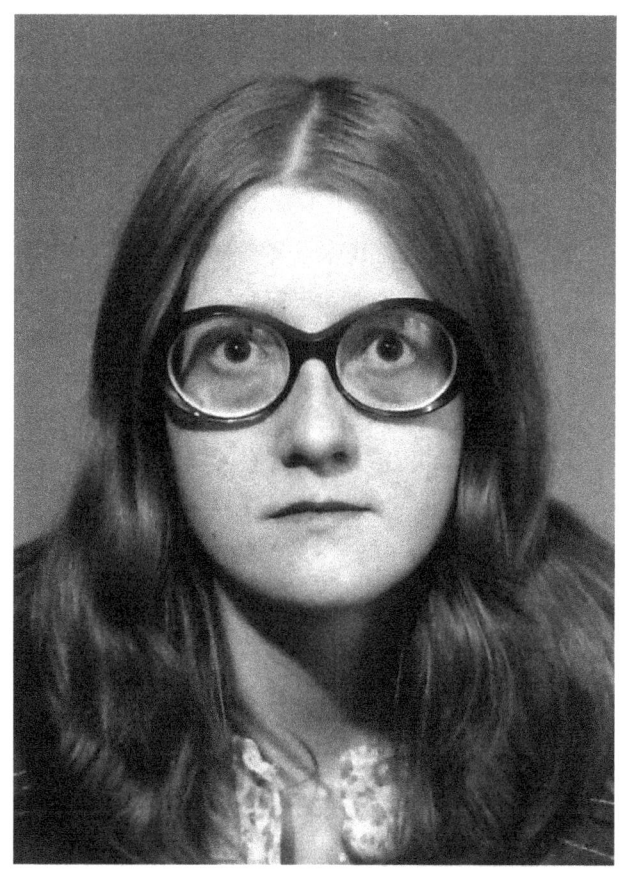

Age 20.

time I wasn't producing estrogen. When I did start bleeding, it was pretty intermittent all the way through until I hit menopause.

In my fifties, I experienced a fracture and broken bones from a cycle accident and a bone density test showed that I had osteopenia. By the time I hit my late sixties, I found out that I had osteoporosis in my lower spine. This came as a total shock to me because I had been regularly running and doing a range of weight-bearing exercises since my thirties. My weight was and still is on the low side, and but for the osteoporosis, my body is what doctors and others call healthy. I also have a low vitamin D count which isn't genetic, but a consequence of my anorexia and the lack of bleeding for all those years.

So now I am having treatment and take Vitamin D daily as well as continuing to exercise. The other thing is that my gut is not the best. I was diagnosed with IBS a few years ago. I'm pretty sure the anorexia would also have damaged my digestive system. The way I look at it now, the damage has been done, but regarding the osteoporosis, I am hoping the treatment I'm following will slow its progress down.

I know I'm not alone here. I don't trust the statistics, but I believe that an inordinate number of women have issues around our body, and our weight in particular. Let's just say that those who don't are definitely in the minority. I don't think it ever truly leaves us. I have seen many older women walking around who are what I call 'functionally anorexic'. I am sure this is at least partly driven by low self-esteem relating to growing older.

Do I still feel like I am one of those women? To be honest, yes, to some degree I do. I keep a check on my weight, but

I no longer do it obsessively. These days I eat healthy plain food and have treats. I mainly think about food when it's time to eat, and I get on with my day outside of that. The major thing that has helped me is ACCEPTANCE of myself as a woman and facing and dealing with all the fears I had back then. It's also about acknowledging that I am not perfect, and in that knowledge, I can now be comfortable in my own skin.

I'm so glad that I am free of the obsession, the guilt, and the shame that possessed me for so many years.

## CHAPTER FOUR

# Leaving The Mothership

It's not hard to work out that I am English if you hear me speaking. I was London born and bred, which to me, is the most boring of accents. There is a huge English diaspora in Australia now, mainly young folks. But way back in the '60s and '70s, the majority of immigrants from the UK came in the form of large contingents of people like me arriving from the UK as Ten Pound Poms.

So there I was in 1969, 18 years old, in the depths of a miserable Manchester winter, hanging over a single bar heater trying to stay warm, when I remembered seeing a poster about a Commonwealth migration scheme to paradise. The choice of destinations included Canada, New Zealand, or Australia. It seemed like a no-brainer to me, especially with the cold getting into my bones in the middle of a UK winter. It literally cost ten pounds to migrate, and all we needed to do was stay for two years to retain our residency. If we chose to return back to the UK within those two years, we had to reimburse the government for the cost of the travel AND pay our way home. Despite this condition, many found that the change in lifestyle didn't really suit them, and took the option of returning home.

Family gathering, 1968.

Family send off to Australia, 1971.

I remembered learning about the Commonwealth in high school and I loved what I saw about Australia. I read all of Neville Shute's books, and a bit of Patrick White, as well as watching documentaries on the Aussie bush and fantasising about becoming a jillaroo deep in the outback. I also imagined falling in love with a jackaroo, as only teenage girls can! Of course, I didn't know I was a lesbian then. So off I went to apply. The brochures were full of photos of paradise. "England by the Beach" it said. Sun, surf, beaches, smiling white faces, new suburbs, schools, and the promise of jobs, jobs and jobs. I realised much later that this was pure propaganda. They wanted white families and young girls to propagate in Australia. I had no idea there was such a thing as the White Australia Policy at the time, and yet there I was in the thick of it.

Little did they know that I had decided never to have kids when I was 12 years old. So, sucked in, Australia!

Plane or ship? We had a choice. It was a no-brainer for me as I had always wanted to go on a ship. In 1971, the family travelled to Southampton to say goodbye to me. I still have a photo of one of my brothers crying his heart out as the ship left the dock.

People said I was brave, adventurous or mad to go alone. But to me, it was a way of escaping England where I was never happy. I was at the start of a new life away from all of my problems. Of course, I was to find out that I took myself with me, but as far as a fresh starts go, I guess I had one.

The SS *Fairsky* was to be my home for the next five weeks. Once the coast was out of sight, I cried for about an hour and that was it. Let the adventure begin. It was a long five weeks of sharing a cabin in the bowels of the vessel with three other single young girls, playing a lot of table tennis, and a LOT of drinking.

As the Suez Canal was still closed, the ship had to go right down to the horn of Africa and turn left at Cape Town. Apartheid was still very real in 1971. I'd watched reports about it on television and never understood why it existed. We had 36 hours in Cape Town, and call me silly, or brave, or any other words that come to mind, but I went into the city for the day via public transport.

Blacks were only allowed on the higher deck, and I decided I would support them by going up to sit with them. I was stunned when I got really blank or angry looks from the people up there. How naïve I was. They were so oppressed that someone like me bucking the system made them fearful. Was I putting them in danger by being there? I will never know because the conductor threw me off the bus.

The ship had more families than singles on it, and way too many kids. After three weeks it got really boring. Our first stop in Australia was Fremantle. I had my first Peters Drumstick there. And two shocks in one go when I crossed the road without using the traffic lights, and got pulled up by a policeman for jaywalking. Worst of all, he had a gun, which frightened the bejesus out of me, never having seen one except on American Western TV shows.

Before long we were on our way to Adelaide, where half of the ship disembarked. I had seen the touched-up photos of the promised land for families in the new suburb of Elizabeth which looked not unlike the housing estate I grew up in. That's pretty much how it turned out to be some years down the track; it had developed distinct similarities to those depressing places in the UK. Yes, I know that Jimmy

Barnes grew up there, but I was headed for Sydney because I had no intention of living in a 'Pommy' ghetto. I could have stayed at home if I was prepared to accept that kind of a life.

The next stop was going to be Melbourne, but we hit the edge of an ocean tornado or some such weather condition and the ship was damaged. The chefs didn't come out of it at all well. Because they had broken their arms when the ship was being buffeted by the tornado, it was Sao biscuits and cheese for two days. We also had to strap ourselves in at bedtime and hold on for dear life to the ropes that had been put up to support us if we had to move to go to the toilet or whatever. I remember sliding from one end of the lounge to the other in my chair. The fact that I was not afraid I can only put down to my drinking!

The amount of damage to the boat meant that we had to spend an extra week in Melbourne, which to me at the time was punishment as it was wet, cold and very English.

Finally, we made our way to Sydney, and I have to say in all honesty, that coming through the heads into the harbour on a spring morning and mooring at Circular Quay was nothing short of magical, and I felt like I was finally 'home'.

Luckily for me, I had been sponsored by my Uncle Ken who moved to Australia when our British Empire family got thrown out of India, and everyone but him fled to England. I didn't have to go to a migration centre because my uncle's family lived in the fairly new suburb of West Pennant Hills and I was going to be staying with them. The first thing my uncle said to me was, "You look just like your mother," and I retorted that he looked exactly like his father. The likeness was indeed uncanny, and for me a bit unsettling.

It wasn't too long before the Pommy bashing started.

First year in Australia, 1972.

I even copped some of it from one of my cousins. I was told in no uncertain terms that I pronounced many of the words I said incorrectly. Like 'yoghurt' and 'vitamin' for instance. Back then I had no idea what a washer or a singlet was, and I thought that being told to bring a plate when going to someone's place for afternoon tea, meant that you literally had to bring an empty plate. So I did. Needless to say, that was pretty embarrassing.

I had my first job within days in a factory, checking hairspray cans. It was my first experience of the old red rattlers, as the trains in Sydney were called back then. The first day when I was meant to be going home to Pennant Hills, I ended up in Pendle Hill, totally lost. My uncle rescued me.

The first beach I visited was Manly. As a redhead with pale skin, I literally burned up to a crisp in thirty minutes. I actually had third degree burns, and I wasn't able to even wear underwear for weeks while the blisters healed. Never again!

As a Pom, I was treated differently. I was told all the time I was a whinger and to go back to England. Indeed there were a lot of English folk who did whinge, and compared everything unfavourably with the way it was back home. Not me, though.

It took me two years to finally feel like Australia was my home, and in 1995 I finally became a citizen. It took that long because the requirement to swear allegiance to the Queen had only just been removed. I have been a British Republican since I was about 10, but even today, voicing a republican bias in the UK is tantamount to treason.

I have been back to England many times and always felt

glad to return to Australia. Yet the last two longer visits were different. I struggled to settle back into my life in Australia when I got home. I kind of fell in love with England again, especially the history, the countryside and all of that, even though in my view, financially and politically it's a bit of a shit hole. While there have been some positive developments, in some ways it hasn't changed at all.

Is it something to do with getting older that I sometimes yearn for the Motherland? Is it a nostalgic, romantic pink cloud I couldn't see when I was younger? I am not sure that starting my life again at 74 is a good idea though. I have created a good life for myself here in Sydney where I am engaged in many communities and politics. Is it a common feature of everyone who chooses (or is forced) to start again in a new country, that we never actually leave our roots? That deep inside we feel a soul connection to the place of our birth?

How the fuck would I know?

CHAPTER FIVE

# Confessions of a (Former) Drug Dealer

Zipping back to 1971, I am 20 and arrive in Sydney as a Ten Pound Pom with the aim of leaving my teenage life of alcohol and VERY illicit drugs behind me, and starting a new life being straight. For the record, 'straight' in this context means being clean when it comes to drugs – not becoming a heterosexual.

For two years, it sort of worked. I was a good girl during the week, living in the suburbs, working, and studying part time. But, come the weekend, it was off to the Cross (Sydney's red-light district in those times) for drugs, sex, and rock and roll.

In 1974 I passed my School Certificate and decided to go travelling for a while. I did a bit of travelling around Australia, picking tobacco in Victoria, then ending up in Cairns, which is in Far North Queensland.

It was the '70s, with the Vietnam War and Woodstock making a mark on the collective consciousness, with David Bowie ruling the airwaves, and hippies like me with our long hair and tie-dyed t-shirts, basically having a great time. Eventually I met up with a few other people and we hitched our way to Darwin. From there we went to East Timor which was still a Portuguese colony at the time. We spent a week literally walking across Timor to Dili. We did all of this with the help of the Portuguese army and lots of red wine.

Then it was off to Bali with its dirt streets, no electricity, no hot water, and only a few tourists who were mainly hippies like me.

Then out came the dope and the magic mushrooms on day one. What's a girl to do, but partake? My straight days were over.

For the next nine months I travelled through Indonesia, Singapore, Malaysia, Thailand, Laos, Burma (as it was then), India and Nepal. There weren't many days when I was straight. Then I hit the opium in Malaysia. That's a whole other story. Suffice to say that I can attest to the fact that it is addictive. I was being reckless in the extreme. I say that because the penalties for getting caught with anything of the sort in Asia were long prison sentences or hanging. But did I care? No!

My first foray into dealing was in Thailand. I got the stupid idea of smuggling bricks of Thai Buddha (that is a very powerful form of cannabis) to sell on my trip. First I had to find it, then buy it, and hide it before moving on. So I asked around and was told where to go, which was an hour's bus ride outside of Bangkok. I met up with some women who greeted me with a cigarette or two. It was only when I smoked them that I realised it was heroin. That was the first of a few times that I tried that drug.

I bought two bricks wrapped in newspaper and got put on a bus back to Bangkok, totally off my face. The bus suddenly stopped and police with machine guns started searching everyone. In my haze, I figured I was fucked. I was the only white person on the bus, so I thought I was going to be sprung for sure.

But they didn't search me, and I found out later that they were looking for gun smugglers. Remember, the Vietnam War was on at the time.

Next, I had to find a way to hide my haul of drugs. I bought a tin of talcum powder, tied the sticks in plastic, and put them in the tin with powder on top. Can you believe it worked?

I tried to sell the stuff when I got to Nepal. The problem was that the talcum powder had got into the bags and they stunk of perfume. Anyway, what fool would take drugs to sell in Nepal when there was plenty there already, but I did manage to sell them!

Unfortunately for me, I ended up getting dysentery twice, and then I was hit with hepatitis A, probably from sharing a bong or three. I actually became seriously ill. With the help of a fellow traveller I managed to get to Delhi and flew back to the UK. I had no health insurance in Australia, and so I had no choice but to return home.

I was extremely thin and very sick when I got back. It turned out that I had also contracted amoebic dysentery, and after a stint in hospital I ended up back at the family home. It took twelve months to recover, and I was told not to drink. But I said to myself, the doctors didn't say not to take drugs. So off I went again, and this time I really went in the deep end.

After I had recovered, I got a job in Manchester with an NGO (Non-Government Organisation) that supplied

## Chapter Five

halfway housing and support for young people coming out of jail. I joined one of the teams and became a resident in one of the houses. My team leader was an ex-member of a '60s group and was a fabulous guitarist. I became infatuated with him. This was in my pre-lesbian days.

Eventually I found out that he was sleeping not only with me, but with about five others, and none of us knew about each other until the whole shebang collapsed.

It wasn't long before the dope came out – lots of it. Then came the acid, speed, cocaine, and then again the heroin. Patrick asked me if I wanted to start selling, and by this time I needed to feed my drug habit, so off I went and started selling. I told myself that if I wasn't putting a needle into my arm, then I wasn't an addict. Only an addict can come up with this kind of justification.

Patrick was using the charity as a cover for a drug ring, and I became entwined in the operation. What was funny but not funny, was that the rules of the hostel were that if anyone was caught with drugs they'd get booted out. Yet there I was, in my room, snorting my head off.

I must say, I was doing home deliveries long before anyone else was, it was just a different product! I got very good at it and started to make lots of money, but my addiction was now all-consuming and I started to do some really stupid stuff. For example, I got mugged at the Manchester University Bar for selling drugs on someone else's turf. The people I was hanging around with at the time carried knives and I saw some pretty violent altercations.

Then I went on a trip with Patrick to Bristol to pick up a big supply and met people who could have been straight out of a mob movie with their dark suits, dark glasses, unsmiling faces, and carrying guns. What the fuck was I thinking? Well not much really – that was the problem.

Of course, the house of cards had to collapse at some point. I was so off my face most of the time, and eventually, I got the sack. Only to go to work the next day and get sacked again because I was in a blackout and didn't know I wasn't meant to be there.

The police were finally onto us and Patrick knew it. By now I was totally paranoid. I threw everything away before the police got me. In the interview, I squealed to save my own skin. The deal was that they would let me go, and that I could leave the country before they did the big bust.

Those last four weeks before I left were full of paranoia and fear for my family. I was so paranoid that I thought I was being stalked by Patrick. I was sure I saw him looking up at me in my window at the back of the apartment block I lived in. I feared that I had put my family in harm's way. I could hardly eat or sleep, worrying that they were going to kill me before I got away. I had no way of knowing if the threat was real, or if the fear I had was the result of paranoia. Speed does that to you. At the end of the day I got away, and my family was unharmed.

I rapidly got back to Australia and my life totally went to shit. I say that because I became a psychotic nutter on the streets. That was when I hit rock bottom in 1977, and I have been clean ever since.

I went back to the UK in 1989 to make amends to those I could find, one being Patrick. It turned out that he had ended up in jail and committed suicide.

All I can say is that the last 45 years have been a journey of leaving all of that behind me, getting help for my addictions, and trying to be a better person. I think I am. I'm not perfect, but I'm doing the best I can.

## CHAPTER SIX

# Hitting Rock Bottom, Finding a Way Back

The fall to the rock bottom of my addiction was a long time in the making, but when I finally reached it I was shattered into tiny pieces.

Where did it start? At 14 my parents had a party at home and the kids' mission was to serve the drinks. All teenagers like to push boundaries, and I was no different. When I collected the empty glasses, I poured all the dregs into a glass and drank it.

What was different for me was not only my physical reaction to alcohol but also my mental state. I had no idea how much 'enough' was, and I drank myself into a stupor. I was told to go to my bedroom and promptly threw up all over the carpet. I don't think Mum ever forgave me for that.

This was the first time, but not the last that I said, "never again". The hangover was shocking and what was worse was the guilt and shame I felt for no obvious reason. Plus feeling depressed for days on end, again with no obvious reason. All of this passed of course, and I didn't drink like that again until I was 17.

Growing up in the swinging sixties in London was as

## Chapter Six

exciting as it was hard. It was a time of great change socially and politically. There were student revolutions, mods and rockers, hippies with their flower power, and rock music. We all thought we could change the world, and we were doing whatever we liked to make the change happen.

When I was 17, the family moved to Manchester when my father got a job there. In the summer, I went on a holiday to St Ives in Cornwall with a few friends. We drank a lot and smoked dope. One night I took the sports car belonging to one of the group without telling him, and drove around the (very narrow) roads in the village. I lost control and smashed the car, panicked and ran away to my B&B. I was leaving the next morning, but the police arrested me before I could leave, and I was charged with taking a car without consent.

I had to tell my parents and naturally they were not impressed. As I was only 17, I had to see a probation officer and then go back to St Ives for the court case. I was told off and cautioned that if I was before the courts again, I would be imprisoned, and then given a fine. That fine took me months to pay off.

Did this experience make me take notice of my behaviour and try and change? NO. Going to the pub underage was common. I would get drunk, and remember one time losing control of my bowels on the way home, and furtively going upstairs to clean myself and my clothes up before making an appearance with the family. I still find it strange that my parents never twigged to what I was doing, especially as I was still living at home.

At this stage I was working at a café in Manchester and started to befriend a young man who came in regularly. His name was John. He told me that he was a registered heroin drug addict. In those days registered addicts in the UK were supplied with a drug called Mogadon. That was the start of my journey to the bottom right there. I didn't know what it was, but that didn't worry me. Such was my desire to try anything. Mogadon (also known as nitrazepam) is a potent sedative, primarily prescribed for insomnia, and in some cases for severe anxiety and even epilepsy.

John would give me a couple of tablets when he came into the café. I ended up in a relationship with John and he introduced me to a whole new world of drugs. I started going to pubs to get uppers, downers, cannabis, and whatever was going, really. Finally I was introduced to acid. What followed from all of this was a quick spiral downwards without me knowing it. I became very shifty and manipulative with my parents and siblings to cover my tracks, all the while becoming more and more secretive. I was dropping acid almost every week and by 19 my brain was pretty fried.

In 1968 I went with some friends to Blackpool to see Small Faces. It was a great concert (what I can remember of it anyway). We drank a lot and got pretty stoned.

After it was over one of the friends took me to the pier and that is where I lost my virginity.

I wasn't aware, of course, at the time, but this was now my pattern. The way it played out was that if I had sex with anyone that wanted it, I would be accepted. The only problem was that mostly, they would walk away and I wouldn't see them again.

That inevitably resulted in shame, guilt, rejection, and a sense of utter abandonment and loneliness. I really wasn't

## Chapter Six

aware of how much self-hatred and low self-esteem affected my behaviour.

Meanwhile, I was trying to be a normal person and joined the Girls Training Corps. I made it to Officer Cadet level and along with several other girls, I went on a trip to Northern Ireland for a two-week camp. This was in 1968 and 'The Troubles' had just started in Belfast. We got out of there quickly and high-tailed it to our camp in County Antrim. Oh dear, I got into trouble again. I was popping lots of those Mogadon pills and giving them to the younger girls as well. Unsurprisingly, when we got back to Manchester, I was told to leave.

Then I really blew it at home. I had taken some pills and to this day I have no idea what they were. I went home and started hallucinating. Seriously, I was seeing spaceships and telling the family all about it. My mother called the police and a doctor. The police searched my room and found all sorts of drugs. The doctor told my mother to ply me with lots of coffee to keep me awake. The next week I was kicked out of home. Did I learn my lesson? Hell, no!

I moved in with some casual friends in 'the Moss' which was a very rundown part of Manchester. I was free to do what I wanted there, and it was a year of total mayhem. It was a life full of alcohol, various drugs, sex and violence, and I started to steal from my workplace to get by.

The flat was a complete mess, with people coming and going all the time. It was crazy, and at times dealers would arrive and there would be fights with knives involved. Casual sex was just part of the deal. I ended up losing my job, and a part of me wanted out.

I got a summer job with a good friend working in a

holiday guest house in Paignton which is in Devon. We had a tiny, shed-like room for our accommodation.

We all went off to the second Isle of Wight Festival in 1970. Over 150,000 people attended. It was one big drug fest, and I was out of my head on acid most of the time. I remember some of the acts, including Free and Jimi Hendrix. I don't think we slept for the whole three days.

My friend was into heroin which I was scared of at that time, though I was taking everything else. One night, her boyfriend turned up and they both shot up. I really wanted to try it, but like true addicts, they were too selfish to share. Their selfishness saved me at that time, ironically. My friend overdosed not long after that, and died at the ripe old age of 21.

I was having casual sex again, and none of it was with a condom. I missed my period one month, and then another month, and I was pretty sure I was pregnant at 18. I was told about a back-door pharmacy where they gave out pills to women who thought they might be pregnant. I visited that pharmacy and took the pills, and to this day I don't know if I was pregnant or not. Regardless, I started bleeding again the next month.

I moved back home and decided to straighten myself up.

I was almost always chronically ill with bronchitis. One day I went to my GP and she must have worked out that I was usually out of it when I saw her, because she gave me a lecture on taking drugs and addiction. I rolled up my sleeves and said that there were no needle marks, so I couldn't be an addict. How arrogant and naïve of me that was, and how very wrong.

This was when I seriously looked at the option of

## Chapter Six

immigrating to Australia with the Ten Pound Assisted Passage option I mentioned earlier. I applied, and eighteen months later I was on a ship to a new life. I thought that if I got away from England, everything would improve. How wrong was I! Among other things, it was very naïve because I failed to understand that no matter where I went, I would be taking myself with me. And I was the problem.

Even the five-week voyage to Sydney was a drunken binge fest. Alcohol was cheap and the bars were open most of the day and night. Nothing at all was changing really, but I was blind to the pattern I was playing out.

Then I hit Sydney and met with my uncle and his family who sponsored me for a few weeks of accommodation on arrival. They lived way out in the suburbs. I felt that this was my chance to start living a 'normal' life.

I tried. I really did try. It was actually quite hard to settle into a new country and way of life. I had several jobs which were easy to come by in the early 1970s. I got a job as a live-in housemaid on the North Shore in Sydney, and made friends with the other three girls in what was a physically heavy job.

I had my 21st birthday there and almost got the sack because I got so drunk. I was celebrating adulthood, and isn't that what celebration was all about? That job finished and I moved back to my uncle's place. That didn't last long as I was a bad influence on one of my cousins and I was told to leave. I found a flat in Harris Park, Western Sydney, and tried again to be a good girl. I got a job in a printing factory, worked diligently, but then got drunk on the weekends. Then I decided to take up part-time study to gain my School Certificate. This involved going to Granville College three

21st birthday, paralytic, 1972.

## Chapter Six

nights a week.

I managed to just have an occasional drink during the week while doing my homework on the four subjects I was taking. Then I would head in to Kings Cross on the weekend to score, and get totally out of my brain on drugs and alcohol, and of course have some casual sex which was a part of the scene. I met a French man and we became lovers and would do acid together. Once I ended up at St Vincent's Hospital on a bad trip and was given a lecture about my drug taking. I took no notice of course as I was convinced it was only 'part time'. Meanwhile, I managed to pass my exams and got a credit in advanced English.

I was asked to keep going and study for my HSC, but I'd had enough of being on the straight and narrow. I was 22 at the time. It's amazing how young bodies can recover and seemingly not bear too many ill effects from overindulgence. However, mentally I was not well. I felt quite isolated and alone – almost disassociated. Once again, I felt that if I changed where I lived, things would get better. So I decided to travel around Australia and see what happened.

This took me to Melbourne for two months, working on a tobacco farm in Myrtleford for three months where I contracted what was called the tobacco disease from all the pesticides that were sprayed in the fields. So I had to leave. Then I hitched my way to Cairns where I met some fellow travellers, and whilst we were not using many drugs, we were drinking plenty of alcohol. After a while, I went off hitchhiking across the country to Darwin, followed by nine months travelling through South East Asia stopping in places like Indonesia, Malaysia, Singapore, Thailand, Laos, Myanmar (Burma), India and Nepal.

Many different experiences were had, but there was one common thread; the drugs that lay at the base of everything I was doing. These drugs ranged from cannabis to mushrooms, to visiting opium dens in Malaysia. FYI, opium has a foul, sickening smell and taste, but that didn't stop me. I smuggled Buddha sticks from Thailand, and then started smoking heroin. In that time my physical health deteriorated, and my mental state wasn't great. I was at risk of getting worse because I felt like I was immune from danger. Alas, I got myself into some really bad scrapes.

By the time I reached Nepal, I was quite thin and sick with my first bout of dysentery. I had to spend another three weeks in Kathmandu recovering before I was well enough to get the local bus to Pokhara.

We came across a landslide on the way, and the bus could go no further. We spent the rest of the day and night in the bus with no food and nothing to drink. A local came by with some chai tea. It was lukewarm and an alarm went off in my head not to drink it. But I was so thirsty that I did, and by the next morning I was sick again. After going behind a wall to empty my bowels I could see blood, and I knew I had yet another bout of dysentery. I had to get back to Kathmandu which was 15 miles away. I had some speed pills that I took, and that got me there. After another two weeks of recovery, I then bussed my way to Pokhara again.

How majestic it was to see Mt Annapurna looking like it was so close that I could touch it. I decided to walk the first part of the Jomsom Trek and set off alone – how silly that was. I got to the first stop and stayed the night. In the morning, I felt really nauseous and lethargic and had to stay in a small guest house for two days to get some strength

Walking back to Kathmandu after landslide, 1974.

back. I got back to Pokhara after a gruelling long hike and checked my pee. Sure enough, the urine was black. This was an obvious sign of hepatitis. I went to the local American hospital where they ran a test and confirmed the diagnosis, saying that I was very sick and needed to leave Pokhara because I wouldn't survive without proper care.

With the help of a couple of friends, I got to Delhi over three painful days. And from Delhi, I got back to the UK. Once I hit Heathrow, I took the train to Manchester and presented at the hospital for Infectious diseases with the note I had been given by the doctor in Pokhara. They admitted me and informed the police of my condition. They went to my parents' home and told them that I was seriously ill. They were shocked as they thought I was still in India. I had decided not to tell them that I was sick and returning home for treatment.

I was isolated for two weeks and then I was released into my parent's care. I ended up being at home for a year because that was how long it took me to recover and put on some weight. Finally, I was back up to 49 kg.

It was three years before I left the UK again. I had to stay at home with my parents for almost a year to recover and get my energy back. I applied for and got my first job as a residential care worker for young people who were in trouble with the law or had drug and alcohol problems.

Once I was back in Australia I was on my own. I felt intense panic and fear about what I was going to do. I landed with a suitcase and $200 in my pocket. I called my parents asking them to send me the money to get back to England, saying I had made a mistake. They said, "No." I went into survival mode and wound up finding a room in a shared

## Chapter Six

house in the inner city of Sydney. Then I started looking for a job. Fortunately I found one at the local public hospital as a mail courier.

The group share house I moved into was a lively place with lots of alcohol and dope available. I started using both again to try and quell the eternal sense of panic that had set in, and I had great difficulties remembering where I was supposed to be. It just got worse every day. I realised that I needed help and a doctor referred me to the Callan Park Hospital to see a psychiatrist. The psychiatrist happened to be blind so I was able to be less than honest about what was going on because he couldn't see my body language, and it was easier for me to lie because of that. He prescribed some anti-depressants that didn't really help.

At twenty-five, I went into a spiral and my drug and alcohol use increased. To say that I was breaking down would be an understatement. My mental anguish was such that I thought I was going to die.

This lasted about three weeks and finally one weekend I called the Callan Park facility and begged them to take me in, as I was experiencing intense suicidal ideation and massive panic attacks. The receptionist put me through to a ward called Mckinnon that, unknown to me, was a detox ward for alcoholics. A nurse took my call and we talked about my situation. She asked me questions about my alcohol use, and I denied I had a problem, but that I had used drugs in the past (omitting to say that I still was). She offered to take me to a recovery program meeting that afternoon, and though I was in denial I said yes because it meant that I wouldn't be on my own.

That afternoon about four women came to my house

and took me to a meeting, followed by another one that evening. I couldn't make any sense of what anyone was saying, nor could I relate to anyone. I thought I was on a different planet to them, but for some strange reason, I got a sense of hope that I could get out of what for me had become a living hell.

The next month was just more of the same, but I did start going to meetings, four a day! My smoking doubled. The reason I buried myself in the recovery program was because for a short while, the panic left me, only to return. Then someone suggested going to rehab. For me, that was just another way of hoping someone or something could fix me. So I quit my job and left my shared house as I went off to rehab. I was only there three weeks, and in that time, I cut my wrists and then left without permission. I travelled to a city station where I tried to jump in front of a train. I was loitering near the end of the platform while I was trying to get up the courage to do it. A guard saw me, and the next thing I knew, I had two police grab me and drag me out of the station and into a car that took me to Callan Park where I was sectioned. I was given lithium in the bum and put on 24 hour suicide watch in a room with a mattress on the floor. I don't know why, and nor did the nurses, but that drug put me out for 24 hours.

When I came to, I was put in a ward and another nightmare began. I really thought I had gone mad in the true sense of the word. All of my imaginings about what a madhouse would be like came true. After three days, I just walked out, and no one stopped me. I went back to the rehab house, but they told me to pack my bags. I kept thinking I had reached the bottom and it couldn't get worse, but it did.

## Chapter Six

I then went to meet with a woman I had met in the meetings and asked her if I could stay with her. She was in early recovery and still struggling herself. This only lasted a couple of weeks as well because she couldn't cope with me and my attacks of fear and panic. So she asked me to leave.

There must have been a spark of willingness to stay alive as I had enough nous to find a furnished room in a boarding house. It had a single bed, a bare globe, a jug, a two ringed stove and a cupboard. Again I felt like I was going to another level of the bottom.

I applied for the sickness benefit as I was totally incapable of working. In 1977, I could just about get through on the measly amount the benefit provided. It helped that all I was doing was going to four meetings a day, smoking heavily and eating cheap, crap food.

I could barely make a cup of tea at the time. This was a low point for someone who was a chef with qualifications from a prestigious catering college in London. Yet there I was, not able to even execute the process of putting a tea bag in a cup, adding hot water, and a splash of milk. It was truly frightening, and added to the sense I had that I was falling into a permanent state of madness.

There were times when I couldn't decide which direction I was supposed to be taking and would walk aimlessly up and down the main street of the inner city suburb I was living in.

I wore shoddy and loose clothes as I was starting to put on weight because I was eating cheap food. Again this was distressing as I had been very skinny (too skinny in fact) over the years of my drug use that went hand in hand with not bothering to eat.

When I went to the meetings, it was the only time I felt a bit safe as I had almost chronic suicide ideation when I was on my own. I thought that I would get out of the hell hole I was in very quickly and go back to being 'normal'. I had no idea at the time that I was actually going through a drug-induced psychosis and physical withdrawal from the drugs and alcohol. I thought I had insects on me and scratched a lot. I also had an unpleasant smell even though I was managing to shower every day.

At the meetings, distressed as I was and unable to sit still for long, I did manage to hear people's stories of their own private destruction and how the recovery program had given them a new life. I didn't relate to personal stories that much at the time. There were a lot of older men and fewer women, and even fewer younger women. What I did relate to though were the negative traits of guilt, shame, remorse, tales of friends walking away, and of feeling utterly alone. I identified with these stories, and being in a room of others in more or less the same boat as me felt a bit safer.

Outside of that environment though, I was constantly in a state of fear and panic. The fear of the unknown (even though living in a state of unknowing is just an everyday state of being for everyone) was the worst panic button for me. If I stopped taking drugs and drinking, what would happen to me?

The question of what I would do if I didn't drink and take drugs was one I couldn't answer at the time. I was 26 and I loved going out and partying. How fucking boring would my life be without drugs and alcohol? Of course, at the time I couldn't see how boring it had already become, with my drug and alcohol consumption at a level that was literally killing me. The truth was that I wasn't actually doing anything with my life except drinking and taking drugs. The irony was lost on me!

After five months of doing this, I could see others getting well but I didn't feel like I was. My madness was still there, I was barely functional, and I didn't see how this was going to help me.

By this time I had seen and acknowledged all of the pits I'd fallen into; all of the casual sex and exorbitant amounts of drugs and alcohol I'd pumped into my body. It was really challenging to acknowledge reality. I had come to see that my life of using substances that were killing me was at an end; I was burned out physically and mentally. But I just couldn't (or wouldn't) see that if I followed what the folks were doing in recovery programs, it would change my life. I wanted *instant* recovery, and of course I wasn't getting it.

I still really didn't recognise how mentally unstable I was, even after five months of not drinking or taking drugs. I thought I understood what being sober was about, and it made no sense to me that I was still living a life full of panic and anxiety. I was really resisting doing what people suggested in the support groups. It all felt so nebulous – words being bandied around like faith, and hope, and your state will pass. I just wasn't getting the fact that addiction and alcoholism are diseases that were still alive in me even though I had stopped using the substances I was addicted to. Stopping using drugs and alcohol was the easy part. But learning how to live without my props was proving to be impossible at that time.

I was in between a rock and a hard place. I knew that my 12 years of drug and alcohol abuse were over, but I just didn't think what the recovery program was offering me was going to work.

I absolutely hated myself, there was no question about that. This hatred had been squashed into my body ever since I was a teenager. The drugs and alcohol covered it up beautifully like they did with a lot of things about my life. I couldn't stand looking in a mirror. How was I going to be able to get over that?

What happened next was the 'sanest' decision I'd ever made. Given the irrational state of my mind, I finally decided that the only way out was to commit suicide and make it work this time.

I went to Kings Cross, which at that time was Sydney's red light district with easy access to drugs. The plan was that I would sell my body, get the drugs, and take an overdose. I had never sold my body in all my years of being a drug user because I made enough money from being a dealer. Given I had lost contact with the dealers I used to use, I could think of no other way to get the drugs. It didn't take long to get a trick, and after the act, I grabbed a bottle of some 30 tablets that were in the room and left. It was the next insane thought I had that actually saved my life.

I was close to the hovel of a room I was living in at the time, but I still had to pass a pub to get there. I thought about buying some brandy to take with the pills which would make it a lethal concoction, but I had been hearing about relapsing in the recovery rooms, and I didn't want to relapse. The irony of the situation was that relapsing isn't something a dead person needs to worry about. Nevertheless, I took the whole bottle of pills without alcohol and was out for almost two days. I came to with someone banging on

## Chapter Six

my door. My life was literally saved by the fact that the people from the recovery program had missed me and came to check on me. To say that I was really angry that I had woken up was an understatement.

I was still alive – had now relapsed – and was back to square one.

What next? I just kept going to the recovery program even though I had slipped back into a state of depression and a sense of nothingness. Then someone suggested that I see an alcohol counsellor at a public clinic. I figured I had nothing to lose, so I went. That was the day I had the first 'light bulb' moment in my recovery journey.

Bunty was her name (now deceased) and she had this beautiful soft Scottish brogue that seemed to calm me down a bit. I think she saw straight through me because after I talked about what I had done, and how I felt like I had fallen into a well with no bottom, she said a couple of things that just woke me up. The first one was that I was very fragmented. Why did that word resonate with my whole being? I just don't know. I do know that for the first time, someone could truly see what my reality had become. It really did seem like I was just a series of pieces of a body with no part working with any other part. I was indeed fragmented. The second thing she said was that I was a lovely young woman, and if I just stopped resisting what the recovery program had to offer, and started to commit to my own healing, I could rewrite my life. She told me that I was a book of blank pages that simply needed to be filled in.

WOW, I literally seemed to float out of that first session with Bunty, and for the first time in many, many years, I actually felt a genuine sense of happiness and I smiled.

I suddenly felt like there was hope, and a way that I could stop the madness that I had sunk into without drugs or alcohol anywhere in the picture.

This happy state lasted about five minutes! But it was enough for me to change my attitude and become serious about my recovery.

I am now 48 years clean and sober… a fucking long time! Nonetheless, it has been 48 years of a roller-coaster ride that has never been linear.

In the first decade, I studied the literature and participated in my recovery. It was then that I started to face my demons. At least as much as I knew about them at this early stage. I became sober and quickly realised I had no idea who I was. I certainly knew what I had become, but who I was? That was a whole other story.

As a kid, I was very curious. I was a daydreamer and a bit of a loner at times, but I was also outgoing as well. I loved walking in nature, reading, history, music, singing, and especially sport which I seemed to be good at. And by my teenage years, I was quite curious about politics. By the end of my drug and alcohol journey, I only had a vague interest in any of these things. They were all superseded by the hazy world I had sunk into.

I started to 'wake up' a little bit and see what was going on around me in the late seventies. But what I had lost was the ability to connect. I had forgotten how to communicate with others apart from offering a grumpy hello or goodbye. I couldn't look people in the eye, and I was extremely awkward and plagued with the feeling that everyone was judging me. It was a very uncomfortable time but at least I was functioning.

## Chapter Six

It took a year or two before I started to feel comfortable enough to spend more than a little while in people's company. I got a job as an office assistant in the public service, which was very simple, but all I was capable of at the time. Having a proper job meant I had to function at some level between 9 am and 5 pm. I felt like I was just going through the motions of living, yet at least I was out there doing it.

One of the first things I realised about myself was that I was a lesbian. It horrified me and was another thing I hated about myself. Society back then was much more homophobic than it is now, so that didn't help me accept myself. I met up with a lot of women in recovery who were also lesbians and that was support I have never forgotten. After three years of internal struggle, I finally accepted that part of myself and was off and running to explore affairs, sex and being with 'my tribe'.

By 28 my smoking habit had increased to forty a day. For a person like me who had chronic bronchitis and asthma, I really shouldn't have ever smoked, but in those days, who listened?

At five years sober I started to explore the idea of getting fit again. I was drawn to the idea of taking up running which was becoming a bit popular in the early '80s.

Meanwhile, after two attempts at quitting smoking and getting a taste for the feeling of being a little bit healthy, I went back to smoking! Then at 3 am one morning I had an epiphany. Up until then, I had gotten into a habit of every day saying no more cigarettes after today, and would deliberately run out. But this particular morning I was feeling so desperate for a cigarette that I started rummaging through the garbage bin for butts. I know this might sound a bit woo woo, but stay with me folks. I suddenly felt like I had floated out of my body and was looking down at myself foraging around in the garbage bin. That's when I saw how insane and addicted I really was.

It took me a few more weeks yet, but eventually, I sought help to stop smoking, using the same recovery program I was using for drugs and alcohol, and I'm proud to say that I haven't had a cigarette since June 1984.

At the seven year mark, I started to have many affairs. This was a whole new experience for me being sober, but I can't really call them relationships because I believed that as soon as the women I was involved with got too close, they would see that I was not a nice person. So before that could happen, I would sabotage the situation and leave the person in question, or be left by them. This became a pattern that played out until I met and fell in love with a woman who was also in recovery. I never thought I would ever have that kind of closeness and respect in my life.

On many levels, it was a confronting time getting to know about being intimate and having to show who I was to another person. This relationship lasted only 15 months because she went back to Canada to live. For my part, I changed my job and became a union organiser for the film and TV industry. I met a woman on a film set who was 12 years younger than me and started another relationship.

I finally felt like I was growing up and experiencing a life that had eluded me for so long. This is no fairytale though, and what happened next shattered me, destroyed the relationship, and sent me once again into an emotional and mental spiral. That experience was to take me on an eight-year journey, travelling through a dark tunnel that I thought I would be stuck in forever. There was no light at the end of that tunnel, I can assure you. And yet I didn't pick up a drink or a drug in that eight years. I might have over-exercised, over-eaten, and been very difficult to be around emotionally, but I never picked up a substance – not even a cigarette.

Those eight years involved dealing with the rape that you'll be reading about in Chapter Eight, and the subsequent volcanic explosion of the impact of my childhood sexual assault. This period felt like I had gone backwards in my recovery. My life was shattered again, and I had literally broken into tiny fragments. To sum it up – I was lost. I can only say that without the help of all the therapists and friends I had, along with the structure of a recovery program, I would have either had a complete and irreversible mental breakdown, picked up drugs and alcohol again, or made sure I didn't stuff up my suicide.

I carried the pain and anger around for all that time. It was really only when I knew there was no answer as to why this had happened to me, and that I could find peace again if I let go of all of the anger I was hanging on to, that the pain started to ease, and I finally saw some light at the end of the tunnel.

I know it might sound twee, but I did develop a faith in something spiritual. To this day I have no idea what it is, but it was having a sense of faith in something outside of myself, that all would be well, that was what helped me climb out of the tunnel.

As each decade of my drug and alcohol-free life has gone on, it has been a journey of coming to know who I am, both

Just sober, 1977.

Still sober, 40th birthday, 1991.

## Chapter Six

the nice parts and the not-so-nice parts. I am not the nasty person who hated her very existence, who could find nothing good about herself except her red hair and blue eyes. I have made many mistakes, had some big challenges, gone back into depression from time to time, moved jobs and houses, participated in many sports clubs, won championships, found wonderful friendships, and stuffed some of them up as well.

There were many amends from my practicing days to make good with family and others, but also in my long term recovery. Just because I was sober didn't mean that I was wonderful to everyone in my circle. Some of my apologies were accepted, some not. Some of the people in question had died or didn't want to hear my amends. I could (and can) only make what I call living amends, to try to be a better person in the world and to give rather than take. Through it all, I have found that I am honest, direct (sometimes too direct!), intelligent, humorous, generous, empathic and care about others. I have found that accepting things I cannot change and just trying to change the things I can is the best way for me to live.

I never ever thought I would find any peace and contentment in my life, and even though it has taken since my twenties to find it, I can never have enough gratitude.

As to how my life has turned out, would I change any of it if I could? Well, yes I would actually, but I cannot, so I try to live in the day to day experience and understand that we are only here for a very short time, and every day is precious.

As the late Joan Rivers said, "I am just glad that I woke up this morning."

Happy days.

## CHAPTER SEVEN

# 1978 and All That

In late 1977 at the age of twenty-six, I finally came out of the closet and acknowledged to myself that I was a lesbian. For years people had been asking me why I spent so much time with women. I didn't know the answer, except that I preferred their company and felt safe with them. I didn't feel any sexual attraction, but then I didn't feel any sexual attraction to anybody at that point of my life.

I had only been in recovery for less than a year, and this was the first time I had the courage to really take a look at myself. I was new to the women's movement (though I had been engaged in women's issues from outside of the tent), and I just liked to keep my distance.

I was starting to meet other women who were in recovery who were also lesbians, and I found them very supportive. I would listen to their conversations but remain distanced.

I truly had an awakening one day. Did I jump for joy and say, "Yeah Sistas!" No fucking way. It was the complete opposite. Growing up I was one of many I'm sure (although I didn't know any) who never wanted to play with dolls even though that is what I always got at birthdays. I wanted what my brothers had. Cowboy suits, toy guns, bows and arrows, and playing football. I climbed trees and mucked

## Chapter Seven

around in dirty pools and played along the River Thames at Putney. I loved sports. I didn't read the Famous Five or fairy stories; I read *Just William* and boys adventure books and comics.

It just seemed to me that boys had more fun and were allowed to do more interesting things. I was what was then called a 'Tomboy'. Looking back can I say I was a lesbian? Who knows? I just think that I didn't want to be boxed into a binary stereotype. Not all lesbians were tomboys, any more than boys who liked to do ballet were gay.

Sadly, I was full of shame and felt dirty; I hated myself for it. I could see with my own eyes how homophobic Australia was. With lesbians, it wasn't so much a case of men being physically violent, but it was about them being violent with their tongues. Name calling and put-downs prevailed. The word *lesbian* was used in a pejorative way. I wanted to hide away, just like I had been doing for many years. But now the door was open, and for me it was never going to close. It took some five years before I fully accepted my sexuality. To this day I find that sad.

There was a support group called Acceptance that I engaged with to talk about my fears and self-hatred. There was also a place called Women's Liberation House that had many groups that resonated with me. I started to attend all sorts of groups including those focused on consciousness raising. This was a time of great political activity within the women's movement. Abortion rights and domestic violence issues were of huge importance. Along with others, I would often be out on the street fighting for our rights.

I had no idea where any of this was taking me, but I found a place where I fitted in with the positive energy of women who felt like me, and who had a political awareness of the issues at hand. I started to make friends in the Women's Liberation Movement, and we would hang around together. It all felt quite exciting.

The weird thing (which I still laugh at today) is the clothes we would wear. High fashion it was not! We wore dungarees, old army pants that were too big, jumpers that were also too big, and in the main we had short hair. I think the idea was to look sexless. The word 'dyke' was a put-down at the time, but we were in the process of reclaiming it. I liked the 'fashion' because I could hide my self-hatred underneath the baggy clothes.

I re-discovered my interest in politics which I had always had since high school, but it had been put on the back burner with other things happening in my life that took precedence. So it felt great to be hanging out with women who I felt were sophisticated and intelligent and appeared to know far more than I did.

Prior to 1978 there were already gays and lesbians actively working towards equality in an organisation called CAMP, which stood for – Campaign Against Moral Prosecution. Some of these activists were involved in organising the International Day of Gay Solidarity on 24 June 1978.

The day started with a protest march from Sydney Town Hall to Martin Place. It was only less than a kilometre in distance but it went through the main shopping area in George Street. We were a moderately sized group but some people did not want to march for fear of being seen on TV.

I found the responses from the Saturday shoppers strange. We either got blank stares or outright verbal hostility. I was absorbing politics like a sponge at the time, and it felt good

Chapter Seven

Morning March. June 24th, 1978. Day of the First Mardi Gras, Sydney. Photo © Sallie Colechin.

International AIDS Memorial Candlelight Vigil, St Mary's Cathedral, 23 May 1994. Photo © C. Moore Hardy, courtesy Australian Queer Archives.

to be part of a crowd of people who thought like me. It also helped me identify myself as a lesbian.

Following this march, a forum on the international gay movement was held at Paddington Town Hall. I heard through the grapevine that there was going to be a protest/celebration that night, and that it was going to be fun. I remember that it was very cold, and I was wearing my lesbian 'uniform' complete with a duffle coat! This was to be my political awakening.

We had one truck at the front playing the music of the time. There was Tom Robinson's 'Glad to be Gay', and Meg Christian singing 'Ode to a Gym Teacher'. These were meaningful songs to those of us in the community. It was refreshing to experience affirmation in any form, rather than the usual put-downs.

We started off with a few hundred people, surprisingly a lot of them were lesbians. This was not always the case, as the gay scene was dominated by men. In fact we had to deal with sexism and misogyny within our ranks (which by the way can still be the case, though less so in some ways).

I was excited to be part of the fun and the exuberant energy felt great. The people on the street didn't know what to make of us, but we didn't care. We were shouting slogans, and I was screaming, "UP THE LEZZOS!" It was all very innocent, but at the same time we were trying to get a serious message across. The message was that we were done with homophobia and wanted equal rights.

We had a police escort full of officers who didn't really want us to be there, and when we reached College Street, it didn't take them long to start pushing us to disperse. But around 10.30 pm there were enough of us in the crowd

## Chapter Seven

feeling determined to get anarchic and march up to Kings Cross. We felt really empowered, which was not something we got to feel very often. So off we went, without police permission, walking down College Street towards William Street on our way to Kings Cross. I saw police vans crossing over the top of William Street towards Darlinghurst Road and thought it was a bit strange, but I didn't really take much notice because I was caught up in the thrilling exuberance of being in a 1,000-strong group of like-minded people.

We carried on to El Alamein Fountain, which is an iconic spot in Kings Cross, and where we had a bit of a chant, and then it was all over. The ending felt like a bit of a fizzer, so we all started to disperse and find our separate ways home. It was only then that it became obvious that we had been ensnared in a trap. There were a lot of police without name tags blocking any exit we could have used. We had nowhere to go, and it turned very ugly. People started to scream as very big burly police, with alcohol on their breath, started to pick us off and throw us into the paddy wagons that were strategically positioned to block off routes we could have used to exit the chaos. Thanks to the police, it turned into a violent riot.

I was hit on my back by the lid of a rubbish bin. I screamed with pain and fell to the ground. There was a lot of pushing and pulling as those who were being grabbed and dragged toward the paddy wagons were also being pulled in the opposite direction by the crowd who were trying to free them. The noise of people shouting and screaming and the slamming of van doors was deafening. That made the environment feel all the more scary. Then it was my turn to be grabbed. Some of my friends tried to pull me back, but the policemen were too strong. I was thrown into a paddy wagon and joined by a few more of the protesters before we were taken to Darlinghurst Police Station.

The men and women were put in separate cells. There were 24 women in the cell I was in, and 53 men in another cell. We were all squashed together, and we were all very scared. That said, it was good to be together. However, one young woman was completely traumatised, screaming that she was straight and that it was a mistake for her to be there. Eventually she was let out. There were other women who had been hurt who were also let out.

The worst part of the night was a guy called Peter Murphy, who for some reason was pulled out of the male cell and viciously beaten. We were powerless to do anything about it, and I can still hear him screaming to this day.

Overnight, we were gradually processed and charged. Someone earlier had told us to give a false name and address. I gave the name of Anne Abbott and joked with the police, asking them what I was going to be charged with. The charge was using unseemly words, to whit, "UP THE LEZZOS."

Outside the police station, hundreds of people had gathered to demonstrate, and we could hear them. Unbeknown to us, money was being raised very quickly to pay for our bail. Back then there were no mobiles or Facebook. It was all done by using an old telephone system and it worked. To say that this was a wonderful thing for all of those nameless people to do for us, can only be an understatement.

The women were then taken to Central Police Station. I was one of the last to be released, at around 5 in the morning. I went back to my home in the Inner West not realising that what happened that night was going to explode in the press and change the whole direction of the LGBTQI community.

I felt really alone on the Sunday. I had no idea what was going to happen, and the experience of the hostile police response in particular, reinforced my sense of being abnormal and hated for a part of me that was just how I was.

We all had to appear at Central Court on the Monday, and the phone trees went into action to get people to come out and support us.

The Sunday papers and all of the TV stations were awash with the news of that night. It was a shock and a disaster for some of the people who had marched to be seen on the TV. Many of us weren't 'out' to our employers or some of our friends. Our sexual orientation was a part of our lives that we had to practice discretion around, ever watchful in case the wrong person should find out.

The New South Wales Premier, Neville Wran, was interviewed and generally sided with the police saying only that some were hurt, and how reprehensible and disruptive we were!

I called my work that morning and pulled a 'sickie' which in a sense wasn't a lie as I was petrified about going to court. What I encountered that morning was equally as distressing. It was a cold and wet day. The front of the Courthouse was full of supporters, but it was hard not to notice the over-the-top number of police officers who were there as well. The press were also there, of course. I started to feel like I was in a circus. Everything seemed to be out of proportion. In my mind, I was just out for a night of fun to affirm that I was a lesbian and that that was OK. But it had now turned ugly in so many ways.

It was very noisy with supporters chanting and clashing with the police. More were arrested. The 53 of us in total who had been thrown in the paddy wagons on the Saturday night were all bailed out. This was just the beginning of what was to be a very long journey of healing. Unfortunately, *The Sydney Morning Herald*, which was the most popular newspaper at the time, printed all of the names of the people who had been called up before the court. This was a decision for which they publicly apologised almost 35 years later. Sadly, it was too late for some who had suffered badly as a result of their privacy being invaded in that way.

I went to work the following day feeling very down. I had a job at the Maritime Services Board in a building that is now the Museum of Contemporary Art at Circular Quay. The statutory body I was employed by was mainly men, and what women there were, were relegated to the typing pool, or like me, they had jobs as an office assistant doing the menial donkey work and being paid much less than the males in the organisation. That was the status quo in 1978.

I could tell when I walked into the office that my colleagues knew I had been one of the people caught up in the fracas that came out of the march. There was much tutting and muttering in the days that followed. I walked around with my head down, did my work, and got out of there as soon as I could. I would make my way home in tears, feeling like dirt.

The next day I was called up to the Human Resources office. My stomach was twisted and I was panicking, thinking that I was about to be sacked. Mike, the Human Resources officer, was very kind. He did in fact tell me that I was supposed to lose my job, but added that he had defended me. He warned me that I had to keep my head down because I wouldn't get another chance. I was so relieved and thanked him profusely. I've never forgotten what he did for me. I found out later that he was also gay, but totally in the closet. He tragically died of AIDS in the '90s.

For about a month after that, I had to endure the kind of homophobia that would be unthinkable and totally unacceptable now. But back then we had to suck it up. Quite often I would come into work and go to my desk and find heterosexual porn magazines of women in various poses and acts when I opened the drawer. I was seriously distressed by this kind of thing, but I could not say anything about it. I just had to put up with it, including the fact that the men were looking at me and sniggering. All of these acts of abuse really wore me down and eventually, I became depressed. This was the difference between being straight or gay. It is something that many of us have had to live with, and sometimes continue to have to deal with for a lifetime.

Thank goodness for our community who didn't get beaten down. Instead, we got angry and moved veritable mountains through strategically planned political action. The following weekend a meeting was held at a hall in Darlinghurst where more protests were planned and organised. There was actually a meeting held with the Premier, Neville Wran. Somehow I was part of the group that met with him, though I didn't get to say anything. One of the people in the group was the relative of a well-known political figure, and I think that freaked Wran out. He certainly listened to what we had to say, but at the end of the day, not much was achieved.

Meanwhile, the protests went on and on. The following one was 15 July. More people turned up in support of our cause and more were arrested. I was lucky that time.

Then on 27 August, the Fourth National Homosexual Conference was being held in Sydney at Paddington Town Hall. In an act of retaliation, the Reverend Fred Nile and his right-wing Christian (and I use that word loosely) Festival of Light group organised an anti-homosexual and anti-abortion rally in the nearby Hyde Park. Needless to say, there were lots of police blocking our way as we marched from Paddington to Hyde Park. Myself and a few others managed to get through the blockades. I ended up being on my own in the crowds. I found what was being said from the dais so ugly and hateful that my emotions took over and I started chanting. But before I knew it, I was assaulted by some of the crowd (in a most un-Christian fashion) and painfully dragged with my arms behind me by two police into a paddy wagon, and once again I was arrested and charged. This time I gave my real name, which proved to be unwise.

I was later arrested at an abortion rally in Martin Place. It was a record year for me with three arrests. Not a bad count I guess, but it took its toll on me. Even though the political push to have the charges dropped from the June and August arrests was ongoing, we still had to appear in court for hearings. I had so many attendances that I am a bit confused now. I do know that I was found guilty of one of the charges. This was when I had the realization that the justice system was not always about the truth, but it was always about credibility.

## Chapter Seven

The police account of my arrest was rubbish. In fact, it was full of lies. I was made out to be a nasty woman with bad intentions who needed to be held to account for my actions (protesting a civil right). I was fined $70, which at that time was a lot of money, and which I didn't have. In my head, I had actually decided not to pay the fine anyway, and went on to disregard every letter I got about it.

Then I got sprung. I was at a hearing and had to do some paperwork under the original pseudonym I used, which was Anne Abbotts. Of course there were always police around when any of us from the infamous riot were in the courts. Unfortunately, as I was signing the paperwork, I heard my real name called out, and like a dumb ass, I turned around and was grabbed by one of the court staff and taken to the cells. So I was being detained for a different arrest than the one I turned up to the court for. I was all alone, and I was terrified. Then a young lawyer who had been helping out the marchers saw me, and paid for my bail and I was able to go home.

Because I refused to pay the fine, I ended up paying it off by doing time at Mulawa (Silverwater Women's Correctional Centre) for four days. Yes, there was the option of doing this back then, and many of us who didn't have much money would do our time, almost as a protest. I only did it once though, and I never wanted to have to go through that experience again.

The precursor to this was that I had a knock at my door on a Monday and two police officers reminded me that my fine hadn't been paid. They told me that I could either pay it very quickly, or go to Mulawa. I was very stubborn at the time and in my mind I was kind of saying, "Fuck you,

I'm not going to give in to any more of your shit." What I actually said was, "Sorry, I'm not going to pay." With that, they advised me to present myself to Glebe Police Station on the Friday.

It was a very weird feeling being treated like a criminal, when I hadn't actually done anything. So there I was in a cell at Glebe waiting for the van to take me to Mulawa along with a few other prisoners. I felt like a low life. We arrived at Mulawa and were put in the remand section overnight.

I was in a cell with three other women. Unlike me, these women were very tough and rough. And I thought I had a shit upbringing! There was one woman who was actually charged with murder. My fear factor went up by 100 per cent when I found that out. When they asked me what I was in for and I told them, they treated me OK. But there was no doubt about the fact that I was at the bottom of the pecking order.

We were given a carton of 200 cigarettes. I had stopped smoking for two years, but I busted open a packet and started again. I then gave away the rest of the carton, trying to stay on the right side of the other inmates. My sleep was pretty fitful that night.

The next morning we were taken to the main area and then into a dormitory before moving on to breakfast. All I can say about the food is that it was SHIT! Yet for the inmates, food was one of the 'joys' to look forward to. It was a highlight in a very dull routine.

What really surprised me, and showed how sexist the system was, was that there were absolutely no opportunities to exercise in the part of the prison I was in. I tried to go for a walk around the perimeter of the outside space we got to

## Chapter Seven

spend time in once a day, but was quickly shoved back to the space in the middle with the others. Why is it only the men who get gyms and other resources to exercise with? It would have definitely helped with physical and mental health issues, and created some positivity in what was a totally negative space.

Once a day we were taken to the grass area and I heard a woman shouting abuse. She was actually in a cage. This was clearly a form of additional punishment. In front of everyone, the prison officers played power games and were negative about everyone. Of course the prisoners retorted and it became part of the game.

I was then ordered to pick up all the cigarette butts that were on the grass, on my knees. These kinds of directions were aimed at demeaning the prisoners as much as possible. It definitely worked on me.

Time went stupidly slowly. The monotony was broken only by meal times and a bit of TV. It was clear to me that many of the women were stoned; either bombed out on antidepressants or on drugs of some other kind.

After a 5 pm dinner, we were locked in our dormitories. I was quite scared of being assaulted by someone just for looking at them the wrong way or saying the wrong thing without knowing it. I had a restless night's sleep.

The next two days were repeats of the first.

I had arranged for a friend to come and pick me up when I was let out on day four. It felt more like four months.

The experience was enough for me to decide that if I was ever fined again, I would just pay it. I had no intention of repeating that awful experience ever again. If prison was supposed to belittle a person, it certainly worked on me.

Among other things, it took me another eighteen months to stop smoking.

I remained politically active around gay liberation. However I had also turned into a fervent feminist and spent more time with the lesbians as I increasingly found that some gay men were still misogynistic, and either sidelined us, or didn't think our efforts had any meaning.

As far as feminism went, I was like a political sponge, soaking up new experiences. It was an exciting time. I read Marilyn French's book, *The Women's Room,* which was a novel that questioned traditional gender-based roles. Then there was Anne Summers' book called *Damned Whores and God's Police,* as well as Rita Mae Brown's *Ruby Fruit Jungle* and *All That False Instruction* by Kerryn Higgs, one of very few Australian lesbian authors who wrote about our lives. These authors opened my eyes to a new way of experiencing the world.

However, there were many cracks appearing within the Women's Liberation space. A group who called themselves Lesbian Separatists emerged who wanted nothing to do with men. This caused a schism with heterosexual women. For my part, I started to adopt the Lesbian Separatist's philosophy.

In the process, I met many lesbians, and my social and sexual life really took off. I had many affairs, and we used to joke about how all of us would have slept with most women in one of our meetings. It was said as a joke, but there was a big element of truth in it.

A women's warehouse was set up in the Haymarket area in what must have been a fire trap – certainly by today's standards. There were four floors and they all had different

## Chapter Seven

groups involved in all sorts of activities. There was a lesbian newsletter, a socialist paper, dances, and even a café which I would help serve in. It was a total community and I relished it. In the early eighties I joined a 'collective' (yes that's the word we used then) to help organise what was a huge lesbian camp out in the bush. The event was full of music, discussions, swimming, sex, alcohol, drugs and music, involving 300 lesbians spending ten days together in the bush. We went around nude thinking we were in Nirvana. It sounds really naff now, but it was a special piece of freedom to me at the time.

We had lesbian pubs and lesbian bands making great music. The most famous venue was RUBY REDS in Oxford Street, Sydney. It was run by a well-known lesbian who was alleged to have been involved in police corruption. In fact, we would regularly see men with short haircuts and big boots come into the club and be given envelopes.

Our community had to be underground because homosexuality was illegal at the time. This left us open to all sorts of corruption. Back then we called ourselves dykes. It was quite binary with people falling either into butch or femme roles, but I had never seen myself as either. The word androgynous suited me better. I was called a baby dyke though because I was recently out and new.

One night I was just enjoying being 'in the scene'. FYI, I am not a dancer, but I enjoy watching those who are, and even though I didn't have an ulterior motive, before I knew what was happening, I had a big butch lesbian with her hands around my throat, shouting, "You dare look at MY woman again and I'll fucking bash the shit out of you!" Then she pushed me down the stairs. Luckily, I wasn't hurt too badly, but I sure learned a lesson that night. Ah, those were the days!

I was also a bit naughty in those days too. A place called KKK's Steam house (now defunct), opened its doors once a month for a lesbian night. This was the '80s and many of us were charting new ways to express our sexuality and many boundaries were pushed. I went to brothels that catered for lesbian sex, with both individual and group options. I had an exciting time paying for sex with a prostitute in my home, which I organised for myself as a birthday present. That felt much safer than going to a brothel. I also got involved in the fledgling S&M scene. I had many sexual adventures (no names, no pack drill). That said, whilst I had an open mind, and understood the protocols, I never really felt safe. There was a lot of drinking and drugging in that scene, and that was not a safe space for someone in recovery.

S&M involves games that play with the notions of having power (over) and control, and it sometimes took me into dark places within myself. It was a place I didn't really want to see, and later on, I found much better and safer ways of dealing with those aspects of myself. In the end, I felt like it was really just too full of falsity and ego driven, and to be honest, it all started to get a bit boring, facile and disconnected from the core of what mattered to me. Basically, it didn't fit with my growing sense of integrity. In saying that, I'm not judging others or myself for that period in my life. It was all part of my journey of discovering who I was as a lesbian. Do I feel shame or regret about the adventures I had? No! Not at all. While I don't go around bringing these adventures into conversation, I am not afraid to be open about it at this late stage in my life.

## Chapter Seven

There are no skeletons in my open closet!

Over time as I matured in my political growth, I realised that for me being a separatist almost meant I needed to keep myself separate from heterosexual women. That didn't fit well with me anymore. Also, the Women's Movement was changing in a number of ways along with the rest of society.

Like a lot of lesbians, I started to get involved again with mainstream gay and lesbian politics. That included the Mardi Gras that honours those of us who marched in 1978 and paid dearly for publicly supporting equal rights for gay and straight people.

Around 1984 there was a growing awareness that gay men were getting ill and dying with an unexplained disease. This was soon to become known as HIV/AIDS. It was a massive blow to our community to see these mostly young men die in such huge numbers.

Unfortunately, this tragedy had the effect of bolstering homophobia in Australia and worldwide. So little was known about this deadly condition from a medical perspective at the time. I personally lost five of my friends, including two women who were drug needle users. Whilst it was mainly men who were taken down by AIDS, there were also women contracting the disease through unsafe sex or using needles. Over time it became clear that it was not just a gay male disease.

The gay newspaper *The Star Observer* used to come out each week with two or three pages full of the names and photos of casualties, mainly men, who had died that week. It was gut wrenching, and caused untold distress and trauma within our community.

In the nineties, I joined the Sydney Gay and Lesbian

Choir and was a member for seven years. There were two really memorable events we supported. The one that is etched in my mind was the candlelight rally and singing we did one Christmas at Ward 17 (the AIDS ward) at St Vincent's Hospital.

The candlelight rallies became an annual event for a few years and thousands would attend. The walk up Oxford Street was silent. We carried candles to shine a light on a tragedy that was almost exclusively being experienced by gay people. It would only have been the coldest, most homophobic people who wouldn't have been moved by this coming together of humanity.

It was also a poignant moment to go from bed to bed, singing carols for those who were so terribly sick. Seeing someone die from AIDS is not a pretty sight, and the memory has stuck with me to this day.

It was kind of ironic really, that the people who came to be the carers of these dying men were a combination of mostly women in the medical profession and female friends. I feel it was this huge crisis in our community that brought us together again, and we learnt (and are still learning) how to cooperate with each other, and put our sexual politics to one side.

The original marchers from 1978 have become known as the 78ers. We have formed our own organization called First Mardi Gras Inc. It has become a way to bring us together again, not just to meet and chew the cud so to speak, but to continue to have a voice within the Sydney Gay and Lesbian Mardi Gras organisation and to create our own events.

Since the late '90s, the Sydney Gay and Lesbian Mardi Gras has continued to grow and change, just like society's values and attitudes around LGBTQI rights have. These days there are many organisations working for equal rights across the spectrum of our community and age groups.

The parade is one night of the year when our community claims the area around Oxford St to remember how we got to where we are now. Instead of 1,000 marching and a few onlookers, the Sydney Gay and Lesbian Mardi Gras now has upward of 5,000 marching with over 300,000 watching along the route, and millions watching in the comfort of their own homes via the worldwide broadcasting of the event. It has become an event that tourists come to see from all over the world.

I love this night and soaking up the atmosphere, hugging the police along the route as a way of putting hate and anger to the side and celebrating what we have grown into as a more accepting and respectful place, with still a long way to go, though. I always find the crowd respectful in acknowledging our part in the history of the parade.

Some of those in our community have voiced concerns about the direction the Sydney Gay and Lesbian Mardi Gras has taken, with the view that it has become too commercial, and the voice of protest has been lost. In particular, there is concern that too many sponsors (and their straight staff) are allowed to march, and more broadly that it has become a massive party devoid of any real meaning.

To some extent, I agree. Yet I can't help but feel proud when I see how happy our young LGBTQI people are when they are celebrating the freedoms we were fighting for back in 1978.

Beyond the popularity of the Sydney Gay and Lesbian Mardi Gras, Australia appears to have grown more

Sydney Gay and Lesbian Mardi Gras Parade, 2022.
With Robyn Plaister and Robyn Kennedy.

accepting of our community, especially when the nation (in a postal vote) showed our politicians that they were in favour of same sex marriage. And on 9 December 2017, the Marriage Act 1961 was updated to define marriage as a union of two people, rather than limiting it to being an arrangement between a man and woman. This became a day of true celebration and many tears of joy were shed, many parties were held, and bookings at the marriage registries all over the country shot up!

For me, it was an accomplishment I never thought I would see in my lifetime, and I was immensely proud of the fact that our protest in what was to become the yearly Sydney Gay and Lesbian Mardi Gras started the process of change that brought us to a place of equality where marriage is concerned.

To the surprise of some (I'm sure) Australia did not collapse. The country went about its daily business. In a sense nothing had changed, but EVERYTHING changed for our community. This was real progress.

Thanks to the work of many of the 78ers over the years who have continued to be active, there is now a committee within the Sydney Gay and Lesbian Mardi Gras which guides the organisation in relation to our presence at the popular Fair Day and also at the Parade. I was on the committee for two years. These days I proudly take my place on the 78ers float during the march, where we're positioned behind the First Nations float.

What does being a 78er mean to me today? It is a strong part of my identity, but it doesn't define me, per se. I have many facets of my life that are just part of being a person getting on with my life and enjoying my later years. That said, I am still a volunteer within the First Mardi Gras team. I love talking to the younger generations who want to know about the history at the Sydney Gay and Lesbian Fair Day. This community day has become huge with over 70,000 coming together in a park in the inner city who are from all walks of life, all sexualities, and all genders who just want to enjoy a day of gorgeousness. I especially love it when I get hugs and am thanked for the efforts we made all those years ago. It makes it feel like it was all worthwhile.

## CHAPTER EIGHT

# Just another statistic

**Trigger warning**
**This chapter contains a description of rape.**

Before I wrote this chapter, I needed to deeply reflect on what to include and what to leave out. Up until now, the only people who knew the full story of my rape were the police and my social worker at the hospital, who was also my counsellor for about eighteen months. I have carried this information around since 1987 because I wanted to protect other peoples' emotions. But as time has gone by, and I have been able to find a place for it in myself, I feel like now is the time to fully disclose what the journey of rape really looks and feels like. I understand why the full extent of the horror is omitted sometimes, yet in a way, I feel like it diminishes the responsibility that men have to understand the consequences of their actions, especially if those who perpetrate the crime of raping another person are never caught and put through the penal system.

The violent cycle of my story is an example which is all too common. Somehow it needs to change, and it is not the women who need to change it. That said, I hope my small contribution will become part of that narrative and contribute to bringing change about. In case you're wondering, I decided to write this chapter in the present tense to give you, my dear reader, a sense of 'being there'.

**The Calm Before The Storm**
It is May 1987. I'm living in Sydney. I have really bad myopia and wear glasses from the minute I get up to when I go to bed. I am 37 years old, a lesbian, and in a relationship with a woman I'll call Sally to protect her privacy. I have been in recovery for just under 10 years. I have not smoked for three years. I live in the Inner West and my partner lives in another part of the city. We have been together for about a year. We are a bit rocky at times, but we try our best to constructively deal with our issues.

I live at the back of a butcher's shop which has two flats that are rented out to people like me. A friend lives upstairs and I live downstairs. The large garden has a high brick wall with a bottle shop on the other side. The entrance to the flats is via a side door. My open kitchen/lounge room has large windows. The week before the night in question on 9 May 1987, I am at home pottering about, as you do on a weekend, and I see a shadow go by my window. Maybe that's a bit strange, but as the owners of the butcher shop sometimes come to get meat out of a fridge that's positioned just outside the entrance to my flat, I think nothing more of it.

My bathroom window is a smallish one that pushes out at the top. So I feel pretty safe leaving it open. Besides, the week before, Sydney had experienced a huge amount of rain and all my washing is strung along my corridor as it needs some air to dry.

## Chapter Eight

Sally is planning to come around and stay the night, however we have a big tiff that afternoon and she decides not to come over after all. Instead, we make peace on the phone. I am menstrual which accounts for my biting tongue. So I spend the evening on my own, together with my three cats, Mary, Sam, and my favourite Blue. She was named after my first lesbian relationship with a woman whose nickname was Blue.

I have a pretty early night, feeling loved and turn in with Blue on my bed. I usually sleep naked at this time of year, and this night is no exception. I turn off the light. What happens next upends my sense of security and literally changes my life.

**The Rape**

I am a light sleeper but because of all the damp laundry drying in the corridor, I have no idea a man has crept in through the small bathroom window. I am asleep but suddenly feel a presence. I know someone is in the room. During the oddly timeless duration of the rape, I have an inner monologue going through my brain that mainly consists of, *Now he is going to kill me.*

I awake to someone blowing in my ears and my name being called. Am I dreaming? No, what is taking place is no dream. In fact, it's a nightmare of extreme proportions. I try to turn around and scream when he says, "Scream and I will slit your throat!" He nicks my throat and cuts my thumb with the knife he brought with him. From then on I am silent except when he talks to me. The only things I'm saying otherwise are to myself in my head.

My intuitive reaction is not to resist. Just to do what he

tells me to. The adrenaline is shooting through my body. I am in total fear, yet outwardly calm. The situation is made worse because I don't have my glasses on.

I tell him that I am having my period and he tells me to pull the tampon out. I have to turn on my back to do this. It is dark, and though I cannot see him, he is so close to my face that I see he has a mask on, and can feel his rough, unshaven skin as he kisses me. His voice is deep and rough. He asks me how old I am. I am frantic. Am I too young? Too old? I lie and say that I am thirty. I now have to pretend that I am heterosexual because I sense that saying I am a lesbian would be the end of me. It could turn out to be a turn-off or a turn-on. I am not to know, and so just keep my mouth shut.

His sweat trickles onto my body. His smell sickens me. Now he proceeds to rape me. He orders me to get onto all fours and penetrates me like a dog. My instinct is to find out where the knife is. I play a game of holding his hand and discover that he has the knife in the other hand. After he came inside me, he lays on top of me and told me he has done this before, and that he hates women and that is why he does it, and that he cannot stop himself. I pretend and try to placate him, telling him it's OK, and that I understand. Inside, I feel intense hate, humiliation, violation, invasion – 'I' disappear as I shrink down inside. I am shivering and tell him I need the doona to cover me as I am freezing. He tells me that I am shivering because of what he has done; that it is the fear making me shiver. He is not wrong.

He then tells me to masturbate him to erection to start again. I start and then suddenly he tells me to roll over and face the wall. This is it, I tell myself. Now he is going to kill me. For whatever reason, he said he was not going to do that, but if I go to the police he will find me and kill me.

He slides off the bed and there is silence. I am too afraid to move for quite some time. Then Blue, my cat, jumps on the bed and cuddles into me. I call out that I am just getting up to get some water. There is no answer. I put on my glasses and put the light on, and slowly walk into the lounge room. He is not there. The door is open. I quickly close it and check out the rest of the flat. He is gone. I go into the bathroom and see a footprint in the bath. That's how he got in. I look in the mirror and I see the deep shock in my face. I look at the clock. It is four am.

**The Immediate Aftermath**
I don't know what to do. I ring my friend Andre (now deceased) who lives in the eastern suburbs and tell her what has happened. She tells me she will be there very soon. In 30 minutes she arrives.

I am in total shock and still nude. She gives me some of my clothes to put on and calls the Rape Crisis Centre, which at that time was only two suburbs away from me. Andre gives me the phone and says the worker wants to talk to me. I take the phone and she tells me her name is Ann, and asks what mine is. I tell her it's Kate and I hear a "Whoa." She asks me if I am Kate Rowe, and I say yes. She tells me it's Ann X, and we realise we know each other through the lesbian community.

She is at my place in ten minutes with a dog. She scouts the back garden to check if the rapist is still around. He is not. She tells me she is going to call the crisis line at Royal Prince Alfred Hospital and that I will be met by Jo Spangaro who is the social worker on duty that night.

Jo is waiting for us in the Emergency department, and we are taken to a private room. By now I feel so incredibly dirty that I want to have a shower straight away. A part of me is thinking that cleaning my body will stop this nightmare. But I'm not allowed to shower until I am examined. A female doctor undertakes the physical examination. I am totally numb. She asks me a few questions and confirms that intercourse has taken place. I am offered medication to calm me down, but I refuse to take it. Because I was in recovery, I didn't want any medication that would pose the risk of me relapsing. This of course meant that I was in a state of hyper-anxiety all the time. The doctor also tells me that as the sex was unprotected, there may be a chance for me to become pregnant and she gives me two morning-after pills to take to alleviate that possibility. I also have to be tested for HIV which was prevalent at the time. I am told that I have to have three tests over six months which gives me even more anxiety, and stress upon stress to deal with.

I am then finally allowed to shower. I stay under the water for what seems an age. I scrub my skin, wanting to scrape away the dirt and shame that I am feeling.

By now it's six in the morning. Jo takes me into her office, accompanied by Ann and Andre, my wonderful support team. I ask Andre to call Sally to let her know what has happened, and ask if I can stay with her. She says yes. For whatever reason, I do not want Sally to come to the hospital.

Jo talks to me in a calm and reassuring manner. I say I am desperate for a cigarette. But I know if I have one, I won't be able to stop. The fear in my stomach is so strong that it makes me want to vomit. Suddenly Jo's phone rings. I scream in a panic. I crumble into a corner and scream some more. I'd reached a point where I couldn't keep my fear and pain inside me. I screamed out, saying that I can't report the matter to the police because he would find me and kill me. In my state of immense fear, I truly believe that this would be the case. Jo tells me that I have a choice of reporting the matter to the police right away, or leaving it for forty-eight hours. I choose to wait. In retrospect, I can see that it would have been better to have reported it immediately.

Ann tells me that the Rape Crisis Centre will stay in touch with me. Jo sets up some counselling appointments with her in the following few days, and says she will call me on the Monday to get my decision about reporting the matter to the police.

Andre takes me to my partner's place. She greets me at the door in tears. She has lit candles. I don't know how to talk. She hugs me. I back away. I can't be touched as the emotional turmoil gets triggered when I am. I feel dead inside, yet I am alive.

I call my workplace and explain to my manager what has happened, and say that I need some time off.

I spend one night with Sally. I'm awake at 4 am. It's like an alarm clock has gone off and I am back in that room feeling all the fear and horror again.

I cannot go back to my home. I ask a dear friend Sarah who lives close by if I can stay with her for a few nights whilst I work out a plan with my support network. She generously agrees. It seems like all I can do is fall apart.

I cannot be alone. Sarah and her household look after me while night after night the mental alarm clock goes off at 4 am, and I am reliving the rape over again.

On the Monday, I contact Jo and tell her that yes, I want to report the rape to the police. She comes with me and two things happen when we get to the police station. I am put in a room with a young female constable who takes my statement. It is very factual, no emotion. Apparently, that's how police statements are made. I am in there for what seems like hours. As I go into more detail, I see this young woman go whiter and whiter. I wonder if this is the first time she has had to do something like this.

Then I am told that detectives have been around to my home to collect as much evidence as they can. I am surprised at the energy these police are putting into capturing the man. I am of no use as I could not see him clearly. But I remember his smell, his voice and the shape of his face. I cannot get those memories out of my mind.

I then go back to the hospital to have another physical examination. Jo stays with me in the room. I have a vaginal specimen taken and the doctor confirms that I have had intercourse and scrapes off some semen to be used as evidence. Through streams of tears, I tell Jo that I don't want this to have happened. *Why? Why? Why?* She consoles me as best she can.

I go to Sally's place and stay there for the night. I can see that she is not coping either, but she is doing her best. I allow her to hug me and fall apart. I have nightmares and wake up talking in my sleep. This is too much for her and for me to bear.

I ask Sarah if I can stay at her place until I sort out somewhere to live. Her household agrees, and I end up staying a month. They are all so caring. I need to keep

## Chapter Eight

the light on all night. I go back to work but only last for two weeks. I just cannot cope. I try so hard to maintain a functional life, yet I have become so totally dysfunctional. The only thing I am able to keep going with is my running. For an hour a day I can be outside screaming at the world, and no one takes any notice really. I go on sickness benefit. I need the light on at night and I am hyper vigilant ALL THE TIME. This makes sleeping through the night impossible. I am very, very exhausted – physically, emotionally, mentally and spiritually.

Then a beautiful thing happens. I am taken to a local park by Sally and find a group of my women friends who had heard about what had happened, and knew I was hitting the ten year anniversary of my recovery. To celebrate that and nurture me more generally, a picnic lunch had been organised. There were hugs galore, flowers, cakes, and beautiful cards. I burst into tears. How can something so destructive happen and then flower into something so caring and loving? We stay at the park all afternoon, and I understood that I am not going to be alone on wherever this recovery journey is taking me.

I find a place in a beachside suburb and it's time for me to go back to my place to pack up. I walk in and a wall of fear surrounds me. The place is filthy with fingerprints and a full search has clearly been undertaken. I pack as much as I can with the help of the friends who are with me, and leave that place for good.

I ask a friend to go and clean the place up and pay her for taking that task off my hands. It's a huge job, and she does it willingly. Any time I have to go to my old suburb, I am fearful that this man will spot me and kill me.

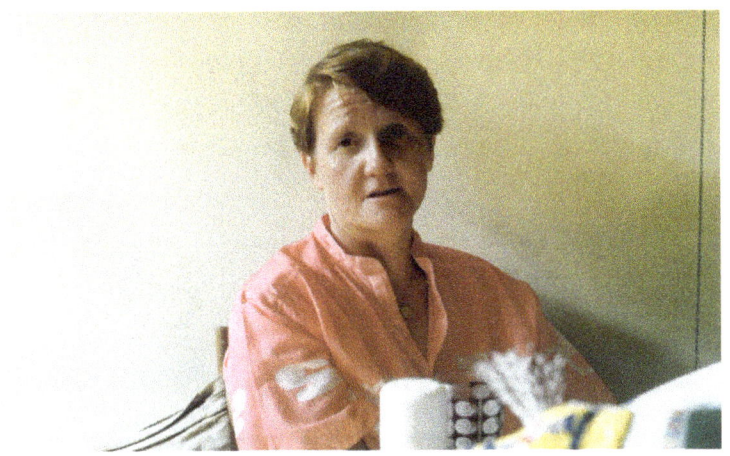

A month after the rape, 1987.

Two years after the rape.
Photograph courtesy of *ITA Magazine*, 1989.

## Chapter Eight

I experience extreme moods swings, nightmares, numbness in my legs, lethargy, and my sleeping is erratic. I cannot get on public transport alone, cannot be around men, and I find myself verbally hitting out at those closest to me. I can't have sex. My brain refuses to be silenced, and I can't stop going over and over that terrible night. I want my life back to what it was – PLEASE. I am totally ripped apart. Will I be like this forever?

I keep running and riding my bike so that I can burn off some of the energy I have building up inside of me, and so that I can scream at the universe. I tell myself not to pick up a drink or drug even though my whole being says that will take the pain away. The destructive part of me says that getting 'out of it' will do the trick. Of course, I know that would be a slippery slope to an even worse place than I am already in, but I am so intensely in pain that I feel like I am going to burst.

Jo suggests I join a rape survivor's support group run by the Rape Crisis Centre. It is a 12 week course. I feel like surely I will be better after that long. Clearly, I have NO IDEA what is in front of me.

What I find is just how many women are violated in all manner of ways. It turns out that rape is common, yet we only hear about the most horrific cases. Like many others, I ruminate on the 'What ifs'. What if I had closed the window (making the whole thing my fault)? What if I had resisted, it wouldn't have happened. What if it had only been oral or masturbation, I wouldn't feel so bad. What if I had put my glasses on, he would have been caught. What if I had told him I was a lesbian, he would have left me alone. What if I had screamed, someone would have heard me or he would have run away. What if, what if, what if – all of these destructive what ifs are so that I can blame myself for the rape.

All of us in the group open ourselves up to the depths of our anguish and support each other in the healing of our wounds as best we can, knowing deep down that we will NEVER be the same.

I have always been a woman who imploded rather than exploded. I keep my emotions in check, but my anger comes out in a passive/aggressive way. Now, I have so much anger that I want to kill, I mean really kill the person who took my sense of autonomy and freedom away. I want to seek revenge because how dare this man destroy my life, how dare he! I have 37 years of pent-up anger in me, and the rape is triggering me to release it. I am so angry at what he has done. I am angry that I had to pretend that I was heterosexual because I couldn't dare risk saying I was a lesbian in case he retaliated in a violent way. I am angry that I am unable to function. I am angry that my relationship has become all about me and the rape. I am angry that I have become so self-centred. I am angry that nothing seems to be able to take the pain away. I am angry that I can't enjoy anything anymore.

The facilitator shows me a way to process these feelings safely. I do that several times in a padded room. The room is empty except for mats, telephone books and plastic piping. I feel so inhibited, but the depth of my anger overrides any awkwardness that might block me from expressing my anger. Once I start, I literally bash those phone books to pieces, all the while screaming at my rapist. It is utterly exhausting and takes me days to get over. And then I repeat the exercise, week after week, until the course finishes. Though this has been so very hard, I know that it has helped me to process my anger and will make my journey relatively easier.

Twelve months later, I apply to the University of Technology Sydney to start a BA in Communications. To my surprise, I am accepted. It is full time, and a part of my attempt to get back to something looking like a normal life. It helps me to have a routine, to focus on something other than the nightmare. To my credit, I am a disciplined person and I really get into the groove of university life.

My relationship with Sally is becoming very difficult, for both of us. We go to couples counselling specifically designed for people dealing with the aftermath of sexual assault. We are told that in most cases, relationships don't survive after a rape. We want so much to prove that wrong, that somehow, we are different. That isn't to be the case, though.

I apply to the Victims Compensation Scheme that is active at that time. Even though there is next to no chance that the rapist will be caught, I figure that I might still be able to get a monetary payment. It is a twelve month process that I could not have done without Jo, my beautiful counsellor, and Sally, who despite everything stays with and supports me. Jo guides me through the paperwork and writes an astonishing victim's statement. Part of what she writes sums up what I have turned into. I've included it below.

"Kate found herself reliving the assault on many occasions and was unable to exercise any control over this. Kate describes losing her sense of motivation. She became listless and sometimes depressed. Her low energy was the combined result of mood swings, constant fears, and lowered self-confidence. Kate's sleeping patterns became erratic. She could only sleep with the light on and would wake up in fear at any slight noise. She had and continues to have nightmares. The troubled sleep regularly compounded the traumatic effects of the rape as she was constantly tired. Her health suffered, and she became run down.

Kate experienced many of the kinds of fears that are well-documented effects of sexual assault. Any outing became a major trauma for her. She described feeling anxious and intimidated by crowds, fearful of dying, fearful of men, fearful of being trapped, fearful of being alone and fearful of dark rooms."

Jo comes with me to court, and I am awarded the maximum compensation, which is $25,000. This compensation money allows me to go back to the UK in the semester break to visit my family for the first time in twelve years. Sally and I leave each other with care, both acknowledging that it is not viable for us to be living together anymore. We agree to deal with this on my return. I am not sure about anything anymore, but I really want us to stay together. I really have no idea how fragile I am.

I am in the UK for 6 weeks. Nana, my paternal grandmother, dies whilst I am there. Sally and I speak on the phone a couple of times before I return.

Sally doesn't meet me at the airport and when I open the door to our flat I immediately know that something big has changed. I can smell incense and see candles in the hallway. There is a card on the dresser. Then I look around and see that literally half the flat is empty, and only my stuff is left.

## Chapter Eight

Blue my beautiful cat comes and rubs my legs, but Jessie, Sally's cat, is gone. It turns out that Sally has left me for another woman that I actually know.

I go into shock, my stomach turns into a tight ball. I fall down on the floor into a foetal position. I cannot move. I feel like I have been violated all over again, feeling abandoned and rejected. There is nothing I can do. I lay there for a long time before I can get up. I cannot sleep. I am racked with turmoil. What do I do?

Trying to let go of the relationship with Sally is so painful. I have become dependent on her for emotional support. Support that she is unable to provide. I have become a drain on her emotional resources. I have become clingy and don't want to be left alone. I have totally lost any sense of personal boundaries. I am unhappy and/or depressed most of the time. In essence, I have just become TOO MUCH.

I cannot eat. Every time I get the emotional wave of pain and panic coming over me, my stomach churns. This is how it is for over two weeks. I lose seven kilos and switch into 'basic function' mode. I have to give notice on the flat and find somewhere else to live quickly. I find a place not far away in the same suburb. I pack up my stuff. All the boxes are piled up neatly in one room. This is my life – boxed in. I arrange for the removalists, unpack my stuff when it arrives, and fall onto the bed with Blue – all but catatonic. Blue becomes my only source of comfort. She jumps up on the bed when I am crying, which is a lot. How wonderful are our pets?

I need to find a flat mate because I still can't live alone. This is immensely frustrating because I have always been an independent person who thrives in having my own space.

I put an ad for a housemate in the local paper. I get a response straight away from a woman who has her own issues. She moves in and we keep our distance. This suits both of us. I move again a few months later into a place in the same suburb with some lesbian friends I met at university.

I am making progress. I am focusing on my recovery. I haven't picked up a drink or a drug through the whole period of recovering from the rape. Finally, I start to get back into a fitness regime; running, cycling and swimming. These are the times when I can feel my body, and be IN my body. It is a good feeling to have, and it's great to be centred, at least for a little while.

In my second year at university, I move into an old flat with two rooms. At last, I can be on my own, albeit still with the light on. I am still in therapy, as the pain and anguish continues. I graduate from university with a major in Film and TV.

I get some casual work at the university working in the media store and on student films. I go to TAFE to learn how to touch type. I get a contract for a year at SBS as a production coordinator in the arts documentary area. I am still having to go to therapy, and at times I get very stressed out. Little things like something left of field triggers me. This is the result of the PTSD. Sally is becoming less and less on my mind even though I bump into her from time to time. When that occurs, it is very awkward because I still haven't totally disconnected emotionally.

Therapy has progressed to the point where I am being encouraged to have an affair or even another relationship. But HOW? I feel like I have a 'post it note' on my forehead, saying HANDLE WITH CARE. A real turn-off in anyone's

## Chapter Eight

language. I take the brave step of approaching a new person, but as soon as the touching starts, it triggers me big time and I am back into the trauma and fall apart again. This is more or less how it plays out on a few occasions. I have to say that all of the women are caring and nurturing, but I just can't seem to get over this hurdle of getting to the point where I can trust that I won't be hurt. I am still so vulnerable, and I am also still angry at times. I back off attempting to establish a new relationship. My whole being is saying, NOT YET.

Then there is the question of men. I find myself hating every man I see. All I actually see are potential rapists. My anger is so palpable that it starts to eat me up. Clearly, I still have plenty of work to do in therapy. I am going about my daily life functioning as best I can, looking for things that are positive, and carrying on with my recovery.

Eight years after the rape, I am still in therapy still dealing with being hypervigilant and experiencing feelings of hate and anger, and of despair around never being able to be intimate again because I am so shut down. I look at couples in the street, observing their intimacy and the way they relate to each other with an unspoken connection, openness and trust. Then I remember that all of those things have proven to be elusive for me. I have put a lot of effort into being fit and healthy because among other things, it is something that is within my control. I still swear at the universe on a daily basis, and I continually ruminate over the "WHY ME?" question that I ask myself over and over, never seeing anything in the way of an answer coming through.

And then I have a huge *aha* moment when the voice in my head says – "WHY NOT ME?" Of course! I finally understand that rape has happened to countless women before me, and it will happen to countless women after me. It is a deeply sad fact, yet this epiphany is all it takes to break me free from my ongoing overwhelming sense of guilt and shame. I realise that I have been asking the wrong question to which there is no answer. I feel like a heavy load has been lifted from me, and I start to feel a bit lighter. It is the beginning of a letting go.

Fifteen years on, and one day I am reading the newspaper and see a story about a rape and arrest. It is still hard for me to read anything like this, but I do, and I go into an emotional spin and get triggered left, right, and centre again. The rape I am reading about is almost exactly the same as mine. I panic – I am right back there again. Is it him? I call Ashfield Police and tell them about my story, suggesting that perhaps this is the same rapist. They take me seriously. I give the police officer the date of my rape. He calls me back two days later to let me know that this particular rapist was in prison at the time I was raped.

At the same time, I ask them to check on my evidence as I knew that a semen sample was taken. They do, and come back with the same disappointing response I'd heard before about all of my evidence being lost, meaning that they are unable to take my case further. I thank them so much for letting me know. I am both relieved and disappointed at the same time. With this, I have a deeper understanding of how the rapist's mind works. It's just a game to them. They all have the same fantasies (some fatal) of power and control through the abuse of women. I get angry, but then see how pathetic and weak rapists are. This is another little moment of letting go for me.

## Chapter Eight

Thirty years have now passed and I find myself reading the paper and seeing that there is a plea for women who were raped in the '80s to come forward because they are trying to find a serial rapist. Again, the accounts of the rapes seem to fit mine and I respond. I get an immediate response from a detective who comes over to my home, and we ended up having a very long conversation. I show her my original police statement. She tells me how frustrated she is because the statement is full of holes, and clearly the new female police officer who interviewed me at the time didn't have the experience to ask the right questions. I then tell her about my lost evidence. She tells me she will check up on it, and I have to hear about the fact that it's a dead end, yet again.

It now turns out that the only way I can move this forward is to fill in a detailed questionnaire, answering it as if I was back in May 1987. I still have that document on my coffee table. I am choosing to leave it be.

Time moves on and so have I. It has taken me many years to have a diagnosis to explain my ongoing symptoms of triggers and episodes of stressing out that seem to come from nowhere. It usually takes me a few days to get over the emotional overload involved. Somehow, it helps to know that panic is part and parcel of my PTSD. I'm kind of consoled when I find out that this is a very common consequence of rape. Knowing this helps me to integrate my trauma into my being. It's easier to accept it than fight the fact that sometimes I get triggered from left field. In fact I still have issues with masks, and when Covid hit, I found it very distressing to have to wear a mask; in fact, I refused in the beginning.

It took me a while to work through this and realise that it isn't just my wellbeing that I have to take into account. I have to wear a mask for the greater good of all. Interestingly, whilst I am still uncomfortable around masks, it doesn't trigger me to the same level of fear as it used to. However, costume and party masks can still be very uncomfortable, but I seem to be able to cope by looking away and having a chat to myself about being safe even though I've been triggered. Most times the sense of panic passes. I don't knowingly go to films that have rape scenes in them. That said, in 2022 when I was back in the UK, the National Theatre Live in London was showing *Prima Facie*. This is a brilliant one-woman play about a young barrister who is raped by a colleague and has to confront how the law deals with rape victims firsthand.

It was a major trigger for me and at the end of the film, I completely broke down. I was inconsolable. It took me right back to the horrors of my experience, with all the pain and grief rising up to the surface again. I couldn't move from my seat. I waited until everyone had gone and went into the toilet. An American woman who was in the audience was still there and she hugged me and let me cry, cry, and cry some more. It went on for what seemed like an hour or more. This lovely woman didn't leave my side until I had calmed down and settled enough to leave the theatre.

It took me about a week to get over that experience, and in that time, I was intensely emotionally fragile and vulnerable. It is when these triggers happen that I can see just how damaged I still am.

I do my best to avoid situations where I feel unsafe. I have developed strong boundaries, and I have learnt to be more open to men. I can even accept hugs these days, yet there is still a gap of mistrust there.

The hardest part of this journey has been understanding and accepting the damage that has been done in terms of trust, and increasing my ability to open up to another human being on an intimate level.

I have avoided this area of my life for so long, and even today it feels like it's a bridge too far for me. When I have felt very connected to someone, it brings up the challenge of trust and the 'What ifs' again. Will I fall apart, will I get hurt again, will they walk away? Even though I have some wonderful close friends who I KNOW I can trust, yet it is still difficult.

People who work in the area of trauma or have been through the kind of things I've been through tell me that it is not impossible to open up again, and I can see that point of view. The thing is that I am a senior person now, and my thinking is that if it hasn't happened before now, it is unlikely to happen.

The other thing is that there is an enormous upside to this. Through being alone and comfortable in my own space after going through years of therapy, it has become just a part of my life experience. I have discovered who I am (good and bad). And I have found contentment in myself. I am alone but not lonely. I have some very solid friendships, mainly with women, but with some men, too. I am not afraid in the world. And I am mostly able to manage the occasional emotional retriggering because I know how to nurture myself.

Against the odds, I have become a very healthy and fit woman, and to this day I remain drug and alcohol free.

I have also regained my love of music and taken up playing the ukulele. What's more, I have discovered that I have a great sense of humour, have a lighter side, and I am sociable and a good friend and confidante. I remain inquisitive, engaged and open to the opportunities that might come up in life, like the opportunity to share my story in a book like this. This is a big deal because it means the experience of being raped no longer defines me, and I no longer hide away.

I sometimes wonder how my life would have turned out if this had not happened to me. But again, this is a question with no answer. It happened. I have survived and done the best I can. I can ask for nothing more. As for the rapist, how sad his life must have been. One thing I know for sure is that he no longer has any power over me.

## CHAPTER NINE

# Same Sex Marriage, Nineties Style

Once upon a time in the dark ages – in 1997 actually – life was different for gay men and lesbians. I know this is hard to believe in this time of enlightenment when we have smartphones, social media, online shopping, Grindr, the Pink Sofa (and whatever the equivalent is for our straight friends), Netflix, and all sorts of other gadgets. But in those days, if you were employed by the state government, superannuation pension schemes were discriminatory in the sense that if you died, your little nest egg could only go to a wife or husband who was in a heterosexual relationship with you. If there was no one who was able to fit this description, then the money was returned to the state.

Since January 2018 here in Australia, where I migrated and still live, the Marriage Amendment Bill was passed into legislation. Every celebrant, dressmaker, decorator, wine store, and wedding cake maker became apoplectic with glee as the queer community queued up to get married. Instead of the state taking our money, we started spending shitloads on weddings.

So, this is a little story of how Ray and I (he was gay, and as you know I'm a lesbian) got married as heterosexuals and why. Ray and I met when I moved into a cheap two-room box (the real estate business calls this an apartment) in Leichhardt, an inner-city suburb of Sydney. It was an old house divided into three flatettes and he lived next to me. We immediately hit it off, and though we both knew we were gay and lesbian, it took a while to acknowledge this to each other. The reason for that was that back then, one had to be a bit more circumspect about coming out because of possible repercussions. In those days closeted and internalised homophobia was almost the norm. Ray had a dog, I had two cats, and as only pets can do, they broke down the distance between us.

Ray was a practising alcoholic, and I was a sober one in a recovery program. I was 12-years sober by that time, trying to make a new life for myself. He would go out at night and come home paralytic. I would find him passed out on my veranda and help him get into bed. He wouldn't remember anything the next day – he was having what's called a blackout.

At least three times a week, he would take his dog out, ostensibly for a walk, but we both knew he was off to visit the local gay beat. I would always say that whatever he did, it was his business, but to make sure that he stayed safe. This was in the days of the HIV crisis when treatments were still hit and miss, and our friends were dying of AIDS *en masse*. The problem was that if he was in, or on the way to being in a blackout, there was no way he could even remember if he had been safe or not.

After I graduated from university, I got a job at a national television station. This meant that I made enough money to move to a better place, which I did. I didn't see Ray for six months, although we kept in contact. Then one day he called me and asked if he could come and visit. I was shocked at what I saw: a very thin man with yellow skin. He had been told he had cirrhosis of the liver and would be dead in weeks if he didn't stop drinking. He stopped drinking immediately. However, his cirrhosis didn't get any better. He decided to retire from work with ill health. He said he was fucked if he was going to let the state get his superannuation, and so he asked me to marry him, which meant that I would get the money if he died.

We went out to dinner to discuss our engagement and the civil marriage requirements we had to meet. It was then that he told me he was HIV+. I knew that at that time AIDS was almost a death sentence. It really surprised me that he was asking me to marry him instead of one of his close straight drinking buddies. It didn't make sense to me then, and it still doesn't make sense to me now. Having lived in poverty on and off for most of my life, being gifted a huge lump sum would literally change my life, so I was happy to enter into this farce of a marriage. We knew we would have to perform the marriage as if we were straight, so off we trooped to the Sydney Registry office – him in a suit and me in a dress. We duly signed the papers and sat through marriage guidance counselling, which was compulsory at the time.

We bullshitted our way through it, and what great actors we were. No one would have guessed the guidance about the deep meaning of marriage, and how commitment should work was totally lost on us. In fact, it's hard to fathom how they got away with being so patronising. Given that

Ray and I getting married, 1995.   Ray weeks before dying, 1997.

we were both in our forties, you would've thought that they would've at least given us an adult-level chat. Of course, the counsellor assumed that we were both straight and that we understood the mores of heterosexuality, which by the way was a long way from the truth of how gays and lesbians relate to each other.

That was when I became aware of the difference between being straight compared to being gay while living in a mainly heterosexual society. To be treated as straight was so different to the experience of being treated as a lesbian. Among other things, my experience of being an out lesbian meant that I became the target of homophobic jokes and verbal abuse.

Before long the wedding day arrived. I had two female friends who were going to be our witnesses. They took me shopping for a nice dress and a girly pair of shoes. I already had a girly haircut, and they did my makeup because, quite frankly, I had always been utterly hopeless with the whole lipstick, eye shadow, powder puff thing. I guess being almost blind without my glasses didn't help. The bottom line was though, that I was not (and am still not) a lipstick lesbian, so being made up at 45 was a whole new experience for me.

We made our vows, exchanged our second-hand rings, and then we had to kiss. This was the weirdest experience, but we rose to the occasion with an Oscar-winning performance. To close off the ceremony, we kissed whilst stifling the urge to crack up laughing. Then we all went off to a reception at the local restaurant, and none of us could stop laughing about how absurd the whole thing was.

After three months with a shared address and banking account that his pension was being paid into, Ray decided to move back to Harvey Bay in Queensland where he was originally from. I hardly heard from him, until out of the blue I received a phone call to say he was very sick and needed help. I contacted the local AIDS organisation in Brisbane and arranged ongoing support for him.

He got worse over the next 12 months, and developed AIDS-related dementia. He wrote to me saying that I had caused his AIDS, that he had fallen in love with his straight counsellor, and wanted a divorce. I, of course, said that it was his money, and he could do what he wanted, and that I would sign the divorce papers after the legal period of twelve months of marriage.

The twelve months came and went, and I didn't hear anything until I got a call at midnight on a Friday from his social worker to tell me that he'd had a seizure and was dying. I had promised him that I would be there for him if this ever happened. At the time, I was a member of a cycling club and had a dear gay friend who I had told about Ray. By that afternoon, he had a return ticket waiting for me at the Qantas counter at the airport. He trusted me that I would pay him back, which I did. I will be forever grateful to that generous man.

I flew up to Brisbane and spent the weekend with him. It was one of the most challenging and confronting two days of my life. To see Ray in agony – and he was in agony – curled up like a baby, blind and skeletal, was nothing short of heartbreaking. According to the nurses, he could still hear me, so I thanked him for the gift that he was passing onto me because it would change my life. I flew back to Sydney on the Sunday night. At 3 am on the next day, I got the call advising me that he had died. I flew back to Brisbane the following week for the funeral, and his few friends were there, along with his dear dog. What was really sad was that his parents had rejected him when he came out and they refused to attend his funeral.

I asked his social worker at the wake why the divorce papers never arrived. He told me that when Ray received my letter stating that it was his prerogative to do what felt right to him because it was his money, he decided to leave it to me because I didn't fight him like he expected me to. Ray's kind act enabled me at the ripe old age of 47 to buy my own little apartment. Up until then, something like this was never going to be anything but a fantasy. It meant that I was able to be financially secure for the first time in my life.

In the '80s and '90s when the AIDS crisis in Australia was at its worst, we were all losing friends on more or less a weekly basis and I reflected on how, in a perverse way, it brought gay men and lesbians together, willing to work towards a more respectful way of interacting. This happened because we stood up to the shared discrimination together, rather than dealing with it as separate communities. We came together on our similarities rather than fighting about our differences. Decades later, some of those differences are still there, and quite apparent, but I feel like we are more conciliatory in our approach towards each other, at least some of the time.

Today, I still wear Ray's wedding ring as well as my own. I do it to remind me to be grateful for what I now have as a result of his generosity, and that, despite our circumstances, we can all share a little kindness that can make a big difference to the people we are in contact with.

## CHAPTER TEN

# Paying it Forward, Almost

Trigger warning.
This chapter contains some explicit medical information.

It's 2006 now. Judith and I met during our recovery journey and became friends. We were both 20 plus years into our sobriety and were very supportive of each other, as good friends are.

I learned that Judith had a congenital kidney condition which was progressive. Being in her late fifties, it was starting to affect her health. Her dream was to have a kidney transplant that would change her quality of life and give her more time to spend with her son and friends. She shared with me what it was like to live with kidney failure which entailed lifesaving daily treatments that kept her bound to a restricted lifestyle.

Judith's condition was deteriorating fast. She started to have peritoneal dialysis. This is a procedure that can be done at home to flush out the toxins that had built up in her system. It required having a permanent catheter implanted into her stomach and flushing it out four times a day. Her belly became swollen, yet she remained a tiny woman. Through it all, Judith kept smiling, and she continued to help other people and practise her Buddhist faith.

We had regular walks and spoke at length about her future while she was looking death in the eye. I found it confronting, but she didn't.

I reflected a lot about Judith, wondering whether I would be able to deal with her condition in the same accepting way that she did. *No,* was my answer. I acknowledged that I was lucky to be a very healthy person who makes sure that I stay that way.

Then I had an epiphany. I spoke to the universe about what I could do. The answer that came back was that I could donate one of my kidneys.

We met up and I made the offer. Judith said that she was on the waiting list but as an older person, it wasn't looking good. So, she had been putting out a plea for donors, but none had come forward. I was the first person to offer which surprised me. It was going to be an uncomfortable and long process, but I was prepared to postpone my plans for the next year if I was chosen. I had to jump through a few hoops first though.

Step 1 involved a blood test. I couldn't believe it when I found out she was O positive. That was great news because we matched, a key requirement.

Step 2 involved meeting my medical team to continue the barrage of tests before the decision could be made about whether I could be a donor or not. Judith had her own medical team that was totally separate to mine.

Step 3 involved heart checks, and what felt like every blood test known to medicine. I did worry about a platelet disorder I have which means my blood doesn't coagulate very well, but my team didn't seem to think this would be an issue, so we continued.

I was very pleased that the nurses and doctors said I was the fittest donor they had seen. I felt chuffed about that, and both Judith and I were feeling positive about the journey we were about to go on together.

Meanwhile, Judith was getting weaker and having problems with her catheter.

The last test I had to pass was a kidney angiogram, and if that was OK, then we would commence the workup for surgery.

Two days after the angiogram, my nurse called and said the doctor wanted to see me. She thought there might be some issue that required me to take a bit of medication for a while or something like that.

I went off to the appointment and the doctor showed me the pictures from the angiogram. I thought about how much of a work of art our bodies are. I was shown a 3D picture that showed every nook and cranny of my kidney and blood vessels. It looked fabulous to me.

Then the doctor gave me the news about what had shown up. Looking at the scan she pointed out that normally there would be one artery for each kidney, and sometimes they see two on one or both kidneys. But in my case, it turned out that I have three arteries on each kidney, this was quite rare. The consequence of that was that the surgeons would have had to alter my donated kidney so that it would work with one artery, which would mean a significant loss of blood. This posed the risk of damage to the donated kidney, and the surgeons weren't prepared to take that risk.

I was devastated and broke down in tears. Surely there must be a way! I knew what this meant for Judith, and I felt

## Chapter Ten

so much grief and a sense of failure. I had some counselling with a nurse and then went home to wait for them to give Judith the news.

I met with Judith a few days later to support her. To this day, her acceptance and lack of anger or resentment is truly inspiring. I asked her if there was anyone else that she could ask to donate a kidney, and she said no. It took me a long time to accept that it was not going to happen.

Within months, Judith got to the point where she needed to start haemodialysis. This entailed her going to the hospital three or four times a week. I could see that she was unhappy about this. I can't begin to imagine what a drain on her energy, both physically and emotionally, this was going to be.

Eventually she was admitted to hospital as the dialysis treatment was not working. She wouldn't let me come and visit her at this stage and I had to respect her wishes.

Then one day Judith called me. She was very matter of fact when she said, "Hi Kate, I am calling you to say goodbye and I don't want you to visit me. I have decided to stop treatment. I have had enough. Thank you for all your support and efforts to help me. Please don't call me again. Goodbye."

And that was it. I called my nurse and told her about Judith's decision. She explained how Judith would die. Apparently, it can take ten days after cessation of treatment. The nurse reassured me that they would make sure she was comfortable, and stressed that she wouldn't be in pain.

Judith died eight days later, in 2008. I was bereft, as were her many friends. She died sober with integrity and humility.

The funeral was in Canberra where her son had settled. In the Buddhist tradition, it was a simple ceremony. There were no photos, no eulogies, no music; it was as if she had never existed. I found this difficult, but I had to accept that was the Buddhist way.

All these years later, I still think of my friend Judith and the lessons of acceptance and faith that she had, and which at the time I didn't yet possess. Seventeen years later, I would hope that in some small measure, I do now practice these two qualities of acceptance and faith. Not in a religious way, but in a spiritual way that reassures me that no matter what happens to us, we are being looked after.

Judith was a dear friend, and I miss her still.

## CHAPTER ELEVEN

# My Best Mistakes

Well, at my age (74), I have had plenty of time to make a shitload of mistakes, and I have definitely lived up to that possibility.

Was it at 12, caring for Candy our guinea pig on the balcony of our London housing estate in the worst winter in English history, and finding her frozen one morning because I hadn't given her enough straw? What's worse, I put her in our oven to see if that would warm her up, but unfortunately (or maybe fortunately under the circumstances), she was already dead!

Or was it at 14, when I was one of the bridesmaids for my Aunt Wendy? It was the first time I had worn heels, and I was so unsteady that I tore the linen of my hired dress.

Or was it at 17, as a cadet officer in the Girls Air Corp when we were on a trip in Northern Ireland and I was caught giving the younger ones drugs and got kicked out?

Or soon after that at 18, giving my brothers drugs and coming home one night so totally off my face that I was seeing flying saucers? My parents had no qualms about calling the police who searched my room and found all sorts of goodies. This got me kicked out of home.

Or was it in my 40s when I was working in admin at a

prestigious university (no names, no pack drill) when I blew the whistle on some dodgy marking of overseas students' work? Next thing I knew, I was served with four pages of allegations against me. That was the beginning of six months of hell having to go to an independent psychiatrist who said I had a borderline personality disorder. Thank goodness for the union, as I ended up getting a payout on the proviso that I signed a non-disclosure agreement. Three years later I happened to meet the Vice Chancellor's PA who told me that I was right, and the person the allegations were about had been sidelined.

Some time ago, I literally bumped into that person at a coffee shop. I recognised her straight away and she sort of recognised me. I said, "Remember me? I blew the whistle on you and I lost my job, then I had a breakdown." She just shrugged and said, "We all did," and then walked away. At the end of the day, it was an emotional time, and I realised that it was going to be best to let it go.

The biggest mistake for me, however, happened 10 years ago. Along with a lot of others, I had lost my job at a hospital when a new administration took over after nine years working there. Previous to that, I had visited Noosa a couple of times, and yeah, like many others, I thought I had found paradise. As a competing triathlete, it was heaven. So I thought – fuck it. It was time for the proverbial sea change. With that, I moved up to paradise, and figured that with my fifteen years working in hospital administration, it would be easy to get a part-time job as an experienced cardiologist EA. So I rented out my little unit, and took my lovely cat Millie with me.

I set about doing what you have to do to move interstate

## Chapter Eleven

– spruce up the unit to get a tenant, engage an agent, book a removalist, downsize everything, calm Millie down because she has sensed that things are afoot, and have a few farewells.

Then it was about looking for a place to rent in Noosa. Without having done much research, I planned to get something close to the beach. So I picked a place in Noosa Heads just ten minutes from the beach, and flew up for the day to check it out. It was positioned under a house that apparently the owners only used once or twice a year. So I signed and paid up, although I couldn't move in for a month. That wasn't a problem because a friend let me stay in his place for that time.

So far, so good. I was getting a bit excited about a new chapter in my life.

It all went smoothly, and the day arrived. Millie was looked after by a friend for a month whilst I made the move to Noosa and settled in. The first month I was there when I was staying with my friend was pretty busy. I was meeting a few triathletes, getting some training in, and starting to look for work. I also got organised to buy a car.

Finally, I moved in a month later and Millie was flown up. I was so glad to see her. Not long after her arrival reality started to bite and things started to go a bit awry. Among other things, I discovered that Noosa Heads is backpacker city, AKA party time – all the time. I don't know how I missed this in terms of the impact it would have on my life, but the establishment next door to my place was a hostel with a loud alcoholic for a manager. Also, the 'once or twice a year' I was told the owner would be in residence turned out to be once a month, and I might as well be living upstairs as far as the penetration of the noise the family made was concerned.

I also found Noosa to be very 'white', with lots of boomers like me – but not like me at all. These folks have lots of money and like to lunch a lot, and not much else. I found it really difficult to find a way in with the locals.

I started looking for a job. I reckon I must have put in over 50 applications over six months while money was going out the door just to cover my basic living expenses. I did manage to get two interviews. Both said yes... then after a couple of days waiting for the details, including my start date, they said no. In one case, the person I would be replacing decided not to leave after all, and in the other case, they decided to employ a student for $10 an hour.

So I thought I would try the hospitality route, being quite happy to take a job like washing dishes or something like that. I would have said yes to anything really, just to bring some money in for a change. I hawked myself around the many coffee shops and restaurants in Noosa, only to find that the youngsters had snagged all of the basic service roles where they were paid a paltry amount under the table.

To make matters worse, Millie took off twice. The second time I just fell apart and realised that I wasn't happy. Fortunately, she wandered back in and saved me from a complete state of despair.

Then on Christmas day, which I spent on my own, I decided to go for a run in the beautiful national park and then have a swim at the beach. So many families were out and about and enjoying the festivities. I swam out a bit, turned over to face the sky, and started bawling my eyes out. I realised I had made a huge mistake, and that I had

## Chapter Eleven

sunk into a depression because I was so very lonely and didn't know what the fuck to do.

My first step was to see a GP because I realised I needed help. Fortunately I wound up getting free counselling. For six weeks I talked and talked and talked, and realised that I had to make a decision because I knew that if I stayed much longer I would have spent half my super with no guarantee of work. I had clocked up six months without having worked a single day.

So I started to look for work in Sydney and planned a trip back for my birthday. I managed to get an interview at a hospital while I was in town. I returned to Noosa and decided to start the process of packing up and returning 'home' to Sydney. It was a big leap of faith, but staying in Noosa would have been a case of killing me softly.

Now this is what makes it right. I set the day and organised the big move back, and once back in Sydney I put my stuff in storage. Before I left, I asked my estate agent in Sydney if the tenant would be prepared to move out early if I paid their expenses. The tenant said yes, and only asked for three weeks rent in lieu of notice. Then, like magic, I got another call from a friend who said she knew a couple who wanted to go overseas for three weeks and asked if I could cat-sit at their place which happened to be in the same suburb my unit. Last but not least, another friend agreed to take Millie while I was cat sitting.

Then on the way from the airport to the cat sit, I got a call from the hospital where I didn't get the job, asking me if I wanted to come in for an interview the following week.

So, in the space of a week, I had gone from total despair to having a temporary place to live before moving back into my unit, and I got a job which was a maternity leave position for nine months, and Millie got to come back to her real home.

How does that work? Coincidence? Serendipity? Who knows?

I ended up losing about $70,000 because of my decision to move to Noosa. A consequence of that was that I had to sell my unit and move into a charity-run retirement village which is like a nursing home at times. Among other things, living here has exposed me to the different ways older people age. Sometimes it seems like I am back in the playground! Let's just say that it isn't the place I would choose to live if I'd had enough money to stay in my unit. But I am grateful to be close to the beach and parks.

Though I have a love/hate relationship with our city, I have a greater appreciation of Sydney after the time I spent in Noosa. The Noosa episode proved that I was human enough to make a mistake, and smart enough to make it right.

## CHAPTER TWELVE

# A Love Letter to Cats

When I was in early recovery from drugs and alcohol in my twenties and very focused on myself, some would have said that I was quite self-centred. To be honest, I would have agreed, and when it was suggested that I should start thinking of and caring for others, I took that on board.

This love letter is to all of those cats who have supported me along the way. Every one of my companion cats became an inextricable part of my life. They actually helped me to get to a place of comfort. I am happy to report that I am no longer as self-centred as I used to be. In fact, these days I know that part of my role in life is about helping others.

Look, some people are drawn to dogs and some to cats. No judgement (really), but I reckon cats are cooler! This love letter is to all of them.

I am about to go all anthropomorphic now and pay homage to dear Blue, Mary, Sam, Simon, Lucy, Sophie, Millie, Rupert, Toby, Charlie and Rosie.

Over the last forty years, all of you have contributed in no small way to my physical, mental and spiritual wellbeing. You have been with me from eight weeks old to 21 years. You have been sadly run over and died in my arms. You have all been rescued from the Cat Protection Society and

Blue

Charlie

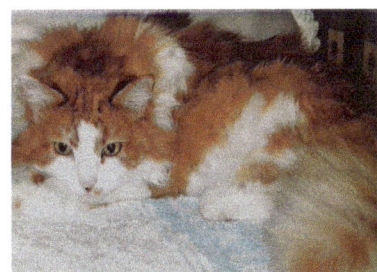

Millie

Rosie

## Chapter Twelve

moggies (cats that do not have a pedigree), meaning that I had no idea what kind of character you would be.

You have been tortoiseshell, ginger, tabbies of various kinds, greys, and black and white.

You have given me so much joy as I played with you, trained you to use the litter tray, thrown away foods you don't like, and given you treats like cheese, milk, yoghurt, and leftover breakfast cereal. I know it's supposed to be a no-no, but hey, how could I resist those pleading little eyes as you purposefully rubbed up against my legs?

You have me laughing out loud at your kitten antics and sudden surges of super-cat energy. Watching you go crazy with the laser pointer is especially comical. Apart from the laser spin toy thingy that eats up the batteries, you all had dozens of different sized balls, both soft and hard, as well as toys of all kinds, and boxes to hide in. So many of them go missing into that hole in the sky, just like the proverbial missing sock syndrome.

Rosie, my current companion, takes the cake in playing catch. I feel like she thinks she is a dog. Since she was a kitten, she has brought a toy of some sort and dropped it at my feet. It didn't take long for her to train me to endlessly throw it for her to bring it back and wait for me to throw it again. One of the things it meant was that I could indulge my lazy side because I didn't have to get up to find the toy so that I could throw it again.

The scratching post was a big FAIL, I'm afraid. Not one of my furry friends EVER used them. But oh, they really love the bed base and the lounge. I call it scratch artistry – what can I say!

You have all been at my side comforting me in times of

stress. When I was totally bereft and in trauma after I was raped in 1987, followed closely by my relationship falling apart, Blue would jump on the bed when I was crying like a baby, and cuddle up to comfort me and sleep with me until I quietened down.

As you read in a previous chapter, in 2014 I made a big sea change and moved to 'paradise' in Noosa. It all went horribly wrong and I fell into a depression. This wasn't helped when Millie my darling ginger cat, went missing one day, and I just fell apart. I was in bed crying like a baby about losing her, then yes, you can guess it, she walked into the bedroom and came up on the bed and comforted me. Cats are like that, aren't they?

You (cats) have annoyed the shit out of me with your biting and misbehaviour. At night, I want to sleep and you want to play!

You have loved being brushed, and you have started World War III if I ever tried to get you to do something against your will.

You have been a total homebody at times and wandered off at others, but you have always come home at night before windows are closed at dinnertime. You have cosied up under the doona at times and stayed as far away as possible from the bed and slept in your own particular spots at other times.

You have let me pick you up and cuddle you, and you have bitten and scratched me at times. I still have the scars.

You have come alive at night when it's time for humans like me to sleep, and you've thrown everything on top of the dresser to the ground.

You have such gross stomach reactions to 'forbidden'

## Chapter Twelve

foods, and I never seem to be able to grab you in time to avoid your projectile vomiting all over my now not so clean carpet. What's more, you still want to play while I clean up your mess. And I clean it up in the full knowledge that it will happen again and again.

You have given me infections and sent me to hospital with cellulitis.

You've found a spot to lounge around on, and almost as soon as I've moved all and sundry for your comfort, you've gotten bored with that one and chosen another spot. And around and round it goes.

You have lived very short lives and been found by someone and returned to me, and Simon and Sophie were found on the road after being hit by a car.

Darling Toby had a seizure and died in my arms.

You have lived long lives, and in the case of dear Millie, made it to the ripe old age of twenty-one.

Lucy went missing for five months. I was convinced she was cat-napped, and fortunately, I got a call out of the blue from a couple who found her in their back garden, five kilometres away from my home. I collected her and as soon as she jumped out of the basket, she went straight to Blue and they rubbed noses. Who says cats have no memory?

You have been healthy your whole life, and you have cost me a bomb in treatments for things like cancer and kidney disease. But not once did I give paying the vet bills a second thought.

You have gone to the vet to be put to sleep. It was always extremely emotional, but the vets have always been caring when it was your turn to pass.

You have been buried in the ground or been cremated

with your ashes strewn, or in Millie's case, they are still sitting on my shelf so that I can remember her forever.

You have all had your own story to tell about being a partner with me. Yes, I admit that I fell in love with some of you straight away, and with some of you I grew to like you despite testing my patience, in some cases leaving me with scars from being scratched and bitten.

When Blue died at the age of fifteen of mouth cancer, and I had to put her to sleep, I experienced so much grief and emotion that I felt it would never leave me. It was a case of dealing with the fact that the real love and companionship Blue filled my life with had gone forever.

Was I a nutter? Was I transferring my lifelong grief onto my cats? Quite likely. However now in my senior years, I can truly say that every one of them gave me far more than I gave them, and helped me along on my journey of healing.

I wrote this poem to Blue, but all these years later, it is the same sentiment I hold for all of my furry friends.

**Beloved Blue**
*After fifteen years together.*
*As we grew to fit each other like gloves,*
*As we grew attached like a pair of old socks or a favourite cardy,*
*I knew that each day with you in my life was a gift of grace.*
*And, as you spent your last days moulded into my lap seeking comfort,*
*I realised I must prepare for your finale.*
*And when that day arrived, I cried. Heaps.*
*And, as I laid you in your lovingly prepared resting place,*
*I knew that I would miss your love and companionship terribly.*
*And I do.*

Some folks love their dogs and humanise them. Cats would NEVER let you do that to them. They are their own master or mistress of their world and having shown them that you can be trusted, will let you into their mysterious planet on their terms.

Our felines are our gift from the universe.

## CHAPTER THIRTEEN

# Deaths in the Family

We are constantly told that there are only two certainties in life – deaths and taxes. How true is that!

So there's nothing unusual about the fact that deaths have been part of my life.

I've lost my maternal grandfather and grandmother, my paternal grandmother, three aunts, an uncle, a cousin, my mother, my father, and a sister.

It is the latter three that were the most difficult ones to experience and had the biggest effect on me. These are the stories of those who were closest to me.

**MUM (Nancy: Deceased at 53)**
Mum had only been in the UK a short while after having to leave India when it gained independence from Britain. She was married in 1948, and in 1949 her first child was born.

There were four children. Helen, me, Peter and Simon, in that order. We were born over a six-year timeframe. We were very poor, and actually homeless when Helen and I were toddlers. Dad was sent to a male hostel and we went with Mum to a female one. Then we got into social housing, first in Woking which is in Surrey, and then

## Chapter Thirteen

Mum, early 20s.

Mum and Dad, 1970s.

London for the next 13 years. We were Catholic, and in the fifties contraception was a no-no. So having sex was like Russian roulette in terms of the potential for pregnancy. In retrospect I don't think Mum really wanted kids, nor do I feel that she was cut out to be a mother. This is not a judgement of her, as I am of the belief that not every woman is de facto a natural mother, but it was the fifties and sixties and women were very much pressured into strict gender roles. If you were a woman, you got married and had babies because that was your role in life. She didn't fit that mould and battled against it. The only problem was that she was a wife and mother, plus she had to work full time. Did she feel stuck and wanted out? I think so.

This letter which my mum wrote in 1971 after her abortion in 1962 is a powerful statement of her experience. I never found out if it was published.

26 March 1971

I had my abortion nine years ago. The psychological conflict which led to the decision was so searing that even today I cannot discuss the subject dispassionately.

We were Catholics and already had four children. By dint of sacrificial self-restraint I had managed to avoid any further pregnancies for seven years. I thought I had reduced the rhythm method of birth control to a fine art when, unaccountably it seemed, I became pregnant again.

Ever since our marriage, my husband's income from his clerical work had been pitiably small, even before the birth of our first child it was only sufficient to pay the rent of a double room and his working expenses. It had therefore fallen on me to supplement our earnings by doing a full-time job and as the size of the family increased, my income became even more essential. I had worked through 15 years and four children with the greatest reluctance, since it meant leaving my small children in someone else's care by day. Because of our concern that the children should remain together and receive the best possible care, this ate up two-thirds of my gross salary. This arrangement made our resources just manageable. Now, the advent of a fifth child would make it impossible for us to gain any economic advantage from my working — and we were faced with the predicament of

## Chapter Thirteen

how to provide for our family. Remember that a working man can make no claims on public funds.

For years I had suffered disparaging taunts and jibes from two sources: from childless people who called me irresponsible and from Catholic acquaintances who said I was wicked to go out to work. However undeserved these judgements were and however much I preserved my composure on public, I was intensely affected by these contradictory pressures and often found my emotional stamina woefully inadequate. Also we had for a short time known the humiliation of homelessness and were determined never to submit ourselves to this degrading experience again.

With the new pregnancy, all my fight deserted me. We had never had a holiday and, when it was not saved for confinements, I had used my annual holiday to earn extra money to introduce the children to experiences which for many of their companions were a routine part of life. In addition, the needs of our children and domestic demands left my husband and I no leisure to enjoy each other's companionship, even though we shared all tasks equally. The thought of all the running we had done just to stand still suddenly overcame me: I felt further effort was futile. Exhaustion took the place of determination and despair replaced hope. I didn't want to deny a new embryo its right to life, but I was already giving all I had to the struggle for existence. I felt incapable of further effort and deprived of the psychological resources I needed to cope with this new event.

Appreciating the needs of children for time, affection and attention, I was aware already that after an endless series of long, hard days I was becoming gradually less capable of giving my children the kind of home atmosphere they needed. I shrank from what would happen to them if the demands of my time, energy and resistance were not stabilised. Caught in the horns of an agonizing dilemma, I could only think of two alternatives: suicide or abortion. The first I found personally preferable; the second did not comment itself to me at all. I made the attempt on my life, but was resuscitated. My doctor said: "It's as well for your young family that you have the constitution of a horse."

His remark, together with my husband's pleas brought me sternly up against the realization that I was not the only person whose life would be affected by suicide. It was only my husband's promise of support in seeking an abortion that enabled me to continue at all.

At his suggestion, I broached the matter with a consultant whom I had to see after cardiac surgery a few months before. I knew nothing would come of it, but because I felt so helpless I allowed myself to be guided by my husband. The consultant was sympathetic,

## Chapter Thirteen

but said simply, "Think how much worse your pregnancy would have been in your former condition." I tried very hard for a week or two to adjust myself to the pregnancy, but my emotional torment became increasingly hard to bear. I approached some women friends for advice on how to get in touch with an abortionist, but they would not or could not help. Someone advised me to ask a chemist in Soho form something to "bring my period on," but the so called abortifacients I was sold had no effect at all. I could not seek a private abortion because we had no means at all, and you cannot have private abortions on an IOU.

In utter despair I phoned a voluntary organisation. In time they referred me to a private psychiatrist who was very kind, but he was not prepared easily to advocate an abortion in my case. I had so far managed to carry an increasingly heavy burden, he pointed out; surely I had the persistence to go through with this pregnancy. I couldn't take this and departed wordlessly. He wrote to me and asked me to be patient. Eventually he sent me to a psychiatric department of a London teaching hospital, where I saw a second psychiatrist. After numerous consultations with my husband, they recommended an abortion.

On admission I was seen by a gynaecologist who refused to perform the operation. I was now more than four months pregnant and felt desolate and abandoned; I had thought my admission to hospital was the end of my struggle and I had foreseen no further setbacks. I threw my wedding ring down the lavatory and watched it disappear. If marriage was nothing but unceasing hard work and emotional strain, I wanted no more of it. Withdrew completely from all contact and miserably awaited my discharge. Ages later, it seemed, another gynaecologist came, but I wouldn't talk to him apart from asking for my discharge. With a gentle compassion which burst my floodgates, he took my hand: "I think you've done your duty by the nation; we can help you." My thankfulness was so great that he had forcibly to disengage himself from my clinging grasp.

I naturally wanted to know what sex my baby was, for he had been viable for some time. But I didn't ask because I wanted to avoid giving the people who had helped me the impression that they may have made the wrong decision. An abortion was not the ideal solution, but given the circumstances, however, I think it was the solution which did least harm to all concerned.

Years later I saw the film "Alfie" and during the abortion scene, I broke down and had to leave the auditorium. I still feel guilt, but I have never doubted that the course I chose was the lesser of two evils. It restored my sanity and my reason; it filled me with

## Chapter Thirteen

fortitude and hope; and as a result I have been able to bring up my children in a happy and relaxed atmosphere.

The children learned about the abortion later. They were very shocked, of course, but I hope one day they will understand how the harshness of reality can sometime impel people to action they would never contemplate in kinder and more tolerable circumstances.

I entreat those who judge the action of others to try and imagine their endurance being tested to the limit; and then to decide if they would have acted any differently. It is very easy to solve other people's problems in the abstract; quite another thing always to make the brave and upright decision in personal problems. Happily, we are not all called upon to subject our tolerances to such a gruelling trial.

Anomie Surd

I was eleven at the time this letter was written, and I knew nothing about the abortion or the suicide attempt, except that she was found in the streets one night and rushed to hospital. I remember the police coming to our flat to tell us about it.

When I was thirteen, she was talking with our aunt Jean who mentioned the abortion when I was in the room. I was shocked and ran out of the room. I was hurt and angry. Not that she had an abortion, but that she kept it a secret.

It was around this time that I made a conscious decision not to have children.

But reading her letter again at this stage of my life, I feel so much compassion for her because I can appreciate how hard it must have been for her, and the desperation she experienced at a time when abortion was still illegal in the UK. My heart bleeds for her when I think about how she must have felt each time she was rejected by the church and male medical practitioners. At least it was fortunate for her that there was a '1929 Infant Life Preservation Act' that meant it would not be an offence for a doctor to carry out an abortion for the sole purpose of preserving the life of the mother, and that she finally found a (male) psychiatrist who could empathise with her plight.

Meanwhile, it wasn't until 1967 that the 'Abortion Act' legalised abortion under certain conditions. The fact is that in many parts of the world the right to make decisions around our bodies still has to be fought for. In fact, what progress has been made in countries like the USA and Australia, is going backwards. Why is it that men in power still want to control women's bodies?

When Senator Kavanagh was in the running to be a US judge, Kamala Harris hit the nail on the head when she asked him what piece of legislation in the US mandates control over a male body. The look on his face said it all and confirmed that in spite of the progress that has been made, some things haven't changed at all!

For whatever reason, my relationship with Mum was intense. I'd go so far as to say that it was symbiotic. We just seemed to clash a lot of the time. Was it my intensity and curiosity as a child that caused this in the beginning?

## Chapter Thirteen

I don't know. I do know that we were in conflict all the way through my formative years until I got kicked out at 17. The catalyst for that was my drug use.

I was very emotional (and still can be) and so was Mum. She was what used to be called, 'highly strung' back in the day. One day she would be so loving and generous and caring, and the next day, in a deeply down mood to the extent that we had to stay away from her. We kids had a code that signalled whether she was 'out' or 'in' on any given day. 'Out' meant it was OK to relax and just be ourselves. 'In' meant it was best for us to stay away. Today this would have been diagnosed as bipolar disorder.

Mum was in a state of despair so much of the time. I was five when I watched her try to jump out of a window after yet another argument with Dad. She was screaming as Dad pulled her back in and I just screamed out of fear. This is a traumatic memory that has never left me. I think my fear of being left by people close to me was set up then. Unconsciously playing out scenarios where I was on the front foot in terms of pulling the pin on relationships before the other person had a chance to, was a pattern I would go on to repeat in intimate relationships for a very long time. There were other times she tried to commit suicide, one of which is recorded in her letter I've shared with you here.

In my teens, when Dad was in Europe working, Mum had many weird episodes. She would stay in bed for days on end, the doctor would come, and Helen and I had to feed her drugs. I remember just feeling so perplexed and distressed to see her that way, not knowing what the problem was and having no one to talk to about it. Our aunts would come around to support her, and yet it didn't feel like we could do or say anything that would acknowledge what was going on. Much of the time, I worried that the way she was, was my fault. For three years Helen and I took on the responsibility of looking after Simon and Peter. Saturdays for Helen and I consisted of washing, shopping, ironing, and cooking. I grew to be a very (almost overly) responsible person.

We didn't have much money, and there were always arguments about that. Both parents had to work which meant that we were 'latchkey' kids. We went to school early and went to after-school care before letting ourselves in around 6 pm.

The truth of it is that as well as having mental health issues, Mum was also not in great physical health. She had her first open heart surgery when I was seven. I prayed that she wouldn't die. I didn't know that she had a mitral valve replaced. In retrospect, it makes sense that whatever mental illness she had, her ill health would have exacerbated it. She became diabetic in her forties. That's not at all surprising given that she used to have three sugars in each coffee, and there was a lot of coffee consumed by her. She was also a heavy smoker and battled with her weight.

When I was about to leave the UK (I was running away actually) to move back to Australia in late 1976, I was told that she would need to have another mitral valve replacement and open heart surgery in the coming months. At this point in my life, I was struggling with my addiction, and it didn't really twig how serious her condition was. To be honest, my own mental illness crisis and being so far away made it easy for me to put everything going on

With Peter and Simon at Mum's grave. Ramsbottom, Lancashire, 2024.

with my mum to one side. That said, we were all keeping in touch via the old-style aerogramme. I had actually written to Mum and Dad about having a breakdown, and let them know that I was trying to do something about it.

In due course, I heard that the surgery was successful and that Mum was recovering well. In fact, she was the happiest she had ever been. Then her mother, my dearest Gran, died in a mental hospital suffering from depression. What killed her in the end was an aortic aneurysm. We all really loved our Gran, and she was a big part of our childhood. My dad made the decision to keep the news from Mum so that she could focus on her recovery.

I felt very distant from Gran's death, and I was very sad about it, but I was glad that I went to visit her in hospital before I left.

In the following six months, the state of psychosis I had been in for a while continued until I worked my way out of it, and started to feel like there was hope for me to recover and start the long journey back to wellness with support. I sent an aerogramme to my parents to let them know that I was starting to improve, but I didn't hear anything back.

I had started a job in late July at the Maritime Services Board and was settling in pretty well. One day I was called out of the office and told that my aunt was outside. That was strange. She asked me if I had received a letter from my dad. I said no, knowing that there was a mail strike on in the UK at the time. She then broke the news to me that Mum had died on August 15. I didn't get the letter about this until three weeks after the funeral.

I left work with my aunt who took me back to stay with

## Chapter Thirteen

her family for a few days. I was in total shock. As soon as I could, I called Dad and asked him why he hadn't phoned me to say Mum had died, and let him know that I would have come back for the funeral. His response was, "Because you would have wanted to come back." I was so hurt by that. I was speechless and terribly hurt about the fact that the decision had been taken away from me.

The actual letter from my father arrived a few days later describing Mum's last few days. She had been well, but suddenly felt weak and her blood pressure became dangerously low. She was rushed to hospital where it was assessed that she had contracted serum hepatitis through the surgery, and it all finally caught up with her and her heart stopped. He acknowledged that he knew that by the time I would have received the letter the date for the funeral would have passed. He also said that he was sure that this would have been what my mother would have wanted. I will never know.

This was a double arrow shot at my heart. I am even more of the view after all these years that my father didn't want to have to deal with me and my emotions, given our difficult relationship.

On a positive note, in another letter I received after the one that knocked me about really badly, Dad told me that Mum had read my letters and commented that I was improving with my mental illness and she was happy to hear that I had got a regular job, and that she loved me. I have never really believed that, even now, but I have a much more mature understanding and have a less judgmental outlook on our (non) relationship. My siblings were also deeply distressed at Mum passing away at such an early age.

In 1989 I was able to make my first visit back to the UK to see my family and make amends to some of those I had hurt in my drug and alcohol days. Because I knew I was going home, and I would be visiting Mum's grave, I created a ritual for myself that I hoped would help me let go.

I wrote her a letter acknowledging that I was very difficult and disturbed, and because of that we were never really able to resolve whatever it was that blocked our hearts from being able to really connect with each other. I also took a candle and then burned the letter. My brothers and sister also came to help clean up the graveside and to spend time in reflection. Helen was very magnanimous in giving me some space on my own to undertake my little ritual, and I cried a lot.

Now, whenever I go back to the UK, it has become a tradition with my brothers (and whilst she was alive, my sister Helen), to visit the grave, clean it up, put in new flowers, and spend a little time in reflection. As time has gone by, I have become more respectful, and to understand how hard her life was while acknowledging that she just did the best she could. It certainly took some time, but I have grown to love her in my own way.

## HELEN (Deceased at 53):

Helen and I were born sixteen months apart. When we were toddlers and before our brothers were born, we got on just fine. We were sent to a Catholic boarding school when I was four and Helen was five. By that stage we were inseparable. Neither of us wanted to be there. Though we were in different classes, we stuck together and shared a dormitory. I have tiny memories of that time. For example,

## Chapter Thirteen

we both got chickenpox at the same time. I remember the green spiral staircase leading to the church where we went every day for Mass. The worst thing was being hit in the back of the legs and on the fingers when we did something 'wrong'. We only stayed for two terms and our parents took us out because of the strict discipline, which today would be called corporal punishment.

Helen and I looked very similar, though my hair was red and hers was a mousy colour. Mum would give us the same haircut and we would share our clothes. In a way we were treated like twins.

We continued to share a bedroom right up until Helen left home to join the Royal Air Force. Looking back on it now, it seems like it was a strange relationship really. I say that because even though we did many extracurricular school activities together, we never seemed to be close like other siblings at school seemed to be.

One good thing was that when we were living in the housing estate which was not a nice place to live, and where we didn't make many friends, we stuck together and played with each other when we were left alone whilst our parents were at work.

As we got older, our differences started to show. As 13 and 14 year olds I loved the Beatles while she loved the Rolling Stones; I wanted the window closed while she wanted it open; I wanted the light on while she wanted it off, and on and on it went.

It got even worse when our parents had the great idea to make our bedroom into a sort of studio so that we would have more space. We were given a sofa bed, so instead of two single beds, we had to share one. It would have been

With Helen aged 4 and 5.

Helen as a teenager.

With Helen, 1988.

## Chapter Thirteen

better if there was such a thing as a King Size bed back then, but unfortunately, that wasn't the case.

When we went on camping trips we always had to be in the same tent and involved in the same activities. Yet with all of this togetherness, we were almost always distant with each other.

For my part, I was actually quite jealous of Helen because I thought that our mum liked her more than me. It wasn't hard to work that out given the way I was treated compared to the way Helen was. That sense of jealousy ran deep for many years.

Helen had her own battles with our parents that I wasn't always aware of at the time. What we had in common was our distress around the family in general, and Mum's mental illness in particular. As we were the oldest, we also had to take care of 'the boys'.

As soon as she could, Helen joined the Royal Air Force and was out of the stifling energy of the family home by the time she was 17. From that time on, I only saw her when she came home on leave, and even then, we didn't spend much time together.

Then I left the UK for Australia in 1971. Helen came with me on the train from Manchester to Southampton where I was going to board the migrant ship. I remember that we did very little talking on the train.

She went on to train as a nurse in the RAF, left the service after a few years, found religion, and went off to Borneo as a missionary, and then onto Zambia where she did a lot of really good work. Then she returned to the UK and chose to become a nun.

A couple of years later, out of the blue, I received a call

from her. She told me that she had left the order because she was having an affair with one of the other nuns. I whooped with joy – not about her leaving the order, but that she came out as a lesbian to me. I had been out for a few years at that point. Finally, we had something in common!

I didn't hear from Helen again until I took my first trip back to the UK in 1989. By then she was in a long-term relationship with her partner Val, and they had bought a house and were living together. I really wanted to see her because I was at a place in my recovery where it was time to make amends for some of the conflicts between us.

I called her to ask if I could stay at her place. She agreed, but only if I didn't talk about stuff in the past. The way she put it was, "If you scratch me, I will bleed." That was very hard to hear but I had to let it go, and realise that many of our past shared experiences would be up for discussion only when she was ready.

We did spend a couple of days together with her partner, and Helen was able to share her own story beyond leaving home, and what she was doing with her life at that time. What really hit home for me was when she said, "It's not that we don't like each other, it's just that we don't understand each other." I was very pleased to have spent that short time with Helen as it turned out to be the last time I would get to see her.

I didn't visit home for some years due to the cost, but I kept in contact with the family by landline which was all that we had back then.

I had taken up competitive cycling and triathlon and was reunited with my love of sport and fitness which has been an important part of my mental, emotional, and physical

## Chapter Thirteen

health. That said, in May 2003, I had a very bad accident in a cycle race and smashed my right wrist and the scaphoid bone in my left hand. I wound up having emergency surgery, and was in plaster for a couple of months. I was unable to work, and fortunately had some insurance which meant that I didn't have to stress about money. In July after the plaster was removed, my wrist collapsed, and I had to go back to hospital for more surgery. I was at home recovering from the surgery when I got a call from Peter, the elder of my two brothers. He asked me if Dad had called me, and I said no. He then told me that Helen had died suddenly. This was a complete shock. He was very upset, and we didn't talk for long, but I said that I would come home as soon as I could.

I still had both arms in plaster and on the Monday when I called the hospital saying that I needed to travel to the UK due to the death of my sister, I was told that I was not able to fly until they had taken the stitches out and re-plastered me, which would be another week.

I called my brother and my travel agent to book a flight as soon as I could. Peter told me that because there was to be a postmortem, the funeral was being delayed. That meant that I could still get back in time for it.

The week before leaving was so painful. I felt the grief of losing Helen suddenly very deeply. I always felt (and still do), that she was a far better person than me, and couldn't see why she had to die and not me. Her death meant that I would not be able to make amends directly to her. Fortunately, my recovery friends supported me in finding another way to start that process. Meanwhile, I bought some dried Australian native flowers and a card to take to the UK with me to put in her coffin.

After a very uncomfortable plane trip with both arms plastered, I went to stay with my sister-in-law. What I feel grateful for to this day is that I was back in enough time to help plan the funeral. I decided to see her body which by this time was starting to decay, as it does. I placed the flowers and the card in the coffin and spoke my amends to her, and kissed her forehead.

I felt honoured to be asked to do a eulogy. There were family members, friends, ex-partners, her current partner, and lots of work colleagues at her funeral. Her decision was to be cremated. I was told that Dad wouldn't be coming to the funeral, but that he would be at the wake. I was saddened, but not surprised to hear this as avoidance of anything emotional was paramount to him.

It was a lovely funeral and wake. I got to hear things about Helen that I hadn't known, including that she had talked to her many friends about me. She was well liked, and it seemed like she'd had many difficulties to deal with that were similar to mine.

Apparently, she was a wonderful midwife. The hardest part of the day for me was that when Dad arrived, he only spent thirty minutes at the wake, including five minutes with me to get a photo and left. I was sad for him that he couldn't cope with being at the funeral, and I felt some anger that after flying across the globe, he could only spend five minutes with me.

A couple of days later we went to an old colliery that was being turned into a massive green space, and we scattered some of Helen's ashes there as it was what she wished. It was literally a case of 'ashes to ashes, dust to dust.'

## Chapter Thirteen

Her long term relationship had ended and she was moving on and into a happier place. Helen was so organised that she had already made her will, and everything went to Peter's children. We siblings were fine with that. I stayed for a couple of weeks after the funeral to visit some of Helen's friends and to be with my family which meant a lot to me at that moment in particular. I spent many days walking in the forests crying, crying, and more crying. Grief appears to be never-ending and at times I still cry and feel a deep sadness.

One day Peter and I went to Helen's house, and he said that I could take anything I liked. I took some CDs of the music she liked, a couple of items of clothing, and some books.

Then I started wandering around her house and I found a notebook. The contents were quite profound. It was kind of consoling to know that she had started to be in a place where she was willing to go to memories of hers that hurt about being in our family. This made sense because she had been attending some 'change your life' workshops. I had (and have) been doing this resolution inner work for years in my recovery path so I understood the journey of healing that Helen had embarked on.

I found a notebook of Helen's with the heading 'RESENTMENTS' on page one. The content of that page was a list of names and mine was on the top. Her resentment took the form of jealousy because I had been Mum's favourite. The paradox was that I had the same resentment, thinking that she was Mum's favourite! And both of us were believing an illusion. I also found out from Helen's partner of seven years, that she was very secretive and didn't want to talk about the past. However, I do know that when her partner became sick with a chronic illness, Helen told her that she didn't want to look after anyone ever again. Why? Because when Mum was having her mental health issues, Helen had to look after all of us as she was the oldest. This was another thing she mistakenly believed, because she hadn't noticed that I was doing a lot of that 'work' as well. So we were both forced into being parents at an early age. Indeed, I also wanted to be free of having to look after family members as a teenager.

What epiphanies I had in the aftermath of Helen's death! Among other things, I realised that rather than uniting us, these joint resentments around the difficult times we had growing up had helped keep us apart for over 45 years. The paradox is, that neither of us were Mum's favourite and we both had to struggle through those years that left us scarred in the same way. Yet we were never able to reconcile our feelings about the experiences we had growing up and beyond.

An inquest was held the following year and it showed no obvious reason why Helen died. She was a healthy 53 year old. The first responders diagnosed the cause of death as Ventricular Fibrillation and she basically flat-lined. The coroner suggested that we siblings be tested for something called Long QT which can cause sudden death, but is not detectable after death.

I returned to Australia and my life. I was under the care of a cardiologist at the time for extreme bradycardia. She tested me in line with the inquest report and confirmed that I was OK on that front.

I made a montage of photos of Helen over her life, and

added the lyrics from the song that was played at her funeral. It was *Deep Peace* by Bill Douglas (1998). There are times when I look at the montage on the wall and when I play her CDs that I weep. I feel like the fact that I cry deeply when this happens is proof that grief never really goes away when someone close to us dies. The way we feel just changes over time.

**DAD (Derek: Deceased at 89)**
When I say Dad, I feel perplexed and distant. He was a mystery to me right up until his death. That was my experience of him for as long as I can remember. Perhaps his own distressing past moulded him into being a distant man, who on the outside was placid and chilled, but was in a lot of pain on the inside.

Dad was sent away to a Dominican Catholic boarding school in Belgium for all his schooling whilst his mother (a singing star in the '30s and '40s) toured to great acclaim. When he finished school, Dad returned to the UK to study for the priesthood at the Dominican Priory near Rugeley in Staffordshire. I can only speculate on why he left. His older brother died of meningitis at 15, along with his father and mother separating when he was young. According to Nana, his father was abusive.

Dad was a highly intelligent man, who was really generous and caring, but he rarely showed any emotion unless it was positive. He was a pacifist and hated violence. Like many of the men at the time, he was called up when WWII was declared. He didn't see active service though and he wound up working in the storeroom on shore in Plymouth.

It was in 1948 when Mum and Dad were introduced to

Dad as a young man, 1940s.

Dad in Australia, 1997.

## Chapter Thirteen

each other. Within three months they were married. Dad had several jobs and I found it interesting to find out that there were different details re employment and addresses registered on our separate birth certificates. They were very poor, and I remember when we were homeless and he was separated from us. I remember the stress both of my parents were under at the time even though I was very young; I know that it pained them deeply to be separated. We were eventually housed on a council estate in Woking which is a town in Surrey.

Being faithful Catholics at that time – when the edict from the church for using contraception was an utter no-no – accounted for four kids to feed, house, and educate. The fact was that they both had to work and life in general was pretty stressful for them.

My memories from my early days at home are of continuing conflict and arguments about money and the stress of life. Mum was emotionally very needy, and a lot of their energy was spent dealing with themselves, rather than us. We were basically left to our own devices from when I was about eight. This coincided with Mum starting to display some of the hallmarks of mental illness. The good thing that came out of this situation is that all of us kids became very independent.

Dad eventually got a decent job in Knightsbridge, London with a business magazine. We got offered the opportunity to move into a flat on a newish council estate in Putney where we stayed for ten years. There were some happy times in those days, though I hated it most of the time. I always felt that Dad was stressed out from trying to juggle looking after Mum and us kids, as well as his job.

He then got another job in Italy, and was away for eighteen months, but he came back for a few days every six weeks to spend some time with us. Mum didn't cope with Dad's absence at all, and when he came home, his focus was on Mum who took up most of the emotional space. We were told that the family was going to move to Rome, and Helen and I were going to boarding school in England. In the end, it didn't happen though, because at the last minute Dad was made redundant. He then got another job in Amsterdam which lasted for eighteen months. Pretty much the same pattern played out with Mum not coping and him coming home to patch things up. Again, Helen and I were meant to be going to boarding school, and again it didn't happen. All of this was very unsettling.

Dad was a great cook. He got a lot of experience when he was working at his uncle's hotel after leaving the priesthood, and did most of the cooking when he was home. A fond memory I have is of him cooking porridge for us while conducting an imaginary orchestra with a spatula while listening to classical music. He loved classical music, and it was our musical mainstay for many years.

I had left school and gone to a catering college in the city at that time. I was in the second year of a three-year course when Dad got a teaching job in Manchester. I wanted to stay in London and finish my diploma, but I wasn't given a choice, so I had to move without finishing the course.

We were finally in a more financially solid place, and in their forties, Mum and Dad bought their first home.

In all of this time, I never really got close to Dad. Meanwhile, my relationship with Mum was pretty toxic, and whilst I know that he tried to understand my point

## Chapter Thirteen

of view, Mum was always his first priority. I must admit I was quite jealous and resentful about that as a teenager. In retrospect, I have to feel for Dad because I wasn't helping matters with my dysfunctional behaviour and excessive drug and alcohol use, not to mention the impact of my anorexia.

So when I decided to apply to be a 'Ten Pound Pom' and migrate to Australia, my parents were all for it and helped me on my way. In those days children seemed to leave home in their late teens or early twenties.

Once I was gone, it seemed to be a case of "We are done, you are on your own now." That applied to all of us, not just me. I kept in contact via letters for many years, but the tyranny of distance made it hard to feel like I was a part of the family.

After Mum died, Dad came to Australia to visit me for three weeks. He mostly stayed with my uncle and aunt and spent a bit of time with me. I took him around the various tourist places, which he seemed to enjoy. Even though he was clearly still grieving, it was one of the rare times when it was nice to spend time with him.

After his visit and a year after Mum died, Dad married again. His new wife was a woman called Laura who he met via a dating agency. By this time I was 27. For some reason, I got a nasty negative letter from her soon after they were married. In it she was venting about my not being nice to dad and not accepting her. It was a very strange piece of communication as I hadn't even met her. I just replied to let her know that as I was 27, I wasn't going to be viewing her as my stepmother, but as Dad's wife. Things kind of went downhill from there really, until Dad died years after he married Laura.

Prior to his death, I made multiple visits back to the UK to visit the family. I organised many dates with Dad, and my brothers Peter and Simon. On all but two occasions, Dad cancelled at the last minute. One of those visits was a quick one that took place at a motorway café. The other was at his home in Skipton. This was actually a nice visit, as long as I didn't talk about Mum.

It turned out that it wasn't only me he cancelled visits with. Both of my brothers made efforts to stay in touch with him, but they were treated in a similar way.

He and Laura were living a very frugal life in a rented cottage in Skipton which is in Yorkshire, and he didn't go out very much. His health had mostly been robust (though I do remember him having dreadful eczema and asthma when we were young), but he was starting to get a few age-related health issues and was stubborn about seeing a doctor.

Distance and time meant that we had huge gaps when it came to opportunities to catch up with him. So our relationship was in a sort of holding pattern. I mainly got news of what was going on with him via my brothers.

Then in early 2014, he started to get quite unhealthy. He developed a foot infection from a podiatry treatment. Laura was also not well, and she was unable to look after him. So he entered a residential care home where he stayed for two years before he died.

He then became so ill that he was placed in hospital and it seemed like he was fading fast. I said to my brothers that I would like to come and see Dad but only if he agreed. He did. So I left within a few days. I was actually training for an ultra-marathon at the time, but of course seeing Dad before he died trumped that.

## Chapter Thirteen

Peter arranged for me to stay at a Bed and Breakfast near the hospital and was at the arrival gate to meet me. At first, I thought that Dad had already died. But instead, he told me that Dad didn't want to see me.

To say that I was angry and hurt would be a complete understatement. I was hurt, because in my view I was being rejected again. I was angry because I'd trusted that he meant it when he said yes. It wasn't so much the money but I had to get permission to take special leave from work, as well as missing the marathon I had worked so hard to be ready for. Anyway, I changed my flight home, and was back within five days.

My brothers then let me know that Dad had improved somewhat and that he was back in the care home.

They say it's an ill wind that brings no good, and I was so full of grief and anger that I ran the first 23 km of the ultra-marathon along the Great Ocean Road in Victoria at record speed. I finished up crying and screaming at the ocean, and ended up completely exhausted (emotionally and physically). I actually had to walk the last five kilometres to the finish line!

I went back to work early with all of that anger and grief still surging around in me. My behaviour did not go down well with my manager. I realised that I needed some help, and quickly applied for access to the employment assistance program which was approved. I spent three months in counselling and accepted that I just had to drop all my vulnerabilities and fall apart emotionally.

The counsellor suggested that I write a letter to Dad. I showed it to her before I mailed it to him. In summary, I let him know how distressed I was about the fact that over the years he had cancelled most of our meetings, and the accumulation of that disappointment meant that I couldn't trust him anymore. I let him know how sad I was that we were never able to have a good relationship and that I couldn't understand why he was not able to be emotionally present. I was also upset about not being able to make amends to him. He wrote back and said he couldn't understand what I was talking about!

And there lay the truth. Life seemed to be emotionally hard for him and so he didn't go there. So it was time for me to let go. Six months later Dad died. I had already decided that I was not going to return for his funeral. I didn't, and I have never regretted that decision.

The thing I felt proud of him for was having an eco-burial at a place in Yorkshire called Tarn Moor Memorial Woodland, just outside Skipton where Dad and Laura lived for many years. It is a beautiful piece of land overlooking the Yorkshire Dales that has been set aside for people to be buried in a natural container. It is for all people, whether they are religious or not. There is no way to identify where he is actually buried because there are no headstones.

Along with visiting Mum's grave, my brothers and I made it a tradition that we would visit Dad as well. The funny thing is that there have not only been many more burials in the field that Dad's body was laid to rest in, but it's hard to actually know where to put our flowers because the woodland has really grown with sheep grazing on the property, and lots of 'rewilding' going on.

I cherish these times with my brothers where we can share some memories of our lives and the times when we were all together. We are all in our seventies now and living

## Chapter Thirteen

'the golden years', though at times it can be tinged with sadness and some regret about Mum, Dad, and Helen. It has taken many decades to come to a place of reconciliation with the past and accept that I cannot change it.

It is time to move on with my own journey.

# Epilogue

So, here we are, wrapping up my parcel of stories I have shared with you.

I know I've shared a lot of tough stuff with you in the chapters that have brought you to this point. So what about the good stuff – the stuff that I can be proud of?

The way I look at things now, I am grateful to have woken up this morning. Everything else is a bonus. If I have learned anything, and I know it might sound twee, it is that every day is precious and there is no time to fuck around. So prioritising my time is a must for me.

I have managed to stay clean and sober for forty-eight years.

I gave up smoking in 1984. That was hard, but because I did it, I'm still able to breathe freely, was able to change my lifestyle, run marathons and triathlons and still stay healthy and fit.

I fulfilled my dream of going to university full time, albeit as a mature age student. I was on the breadline (and sometimes below it), delivering pizzas to make ends meet, and stacked on the weight in the process. But I finished and achieved a BA in Communication, majoring in Film and TV, and had an (albeit short) career out of it. I was told by

Graduating University of Technology, Sydney, 1991.

In Antarctica, 2019.

## Epilogue

some of my lecturers that I had a skill in writing, and I had a couple of things published. But a lack of belief in myself meant that I didn't believe them, so I missed that calling. Writing this book sort of makes up for it, I guess.

I joined the Sydney Gay and Lesbian Choir for seven years, and what fun it was to perform (a childhood fantasy of mine). I also found that I had a decent soprano voice and could harmonise pretty well. Two great memories of that time were entering a national competition that was held in Wagga Wagga as part of an openly gay and lesbian choir – and winning. And performing at the Sydney Gay and Lesbian Mardi Gras Party as the final act with Julian Cleary as the star act in front of 10,000 drunk and drug-fucked gays and lesbians at 10 am on a Sunday morning, was well – a *unique experience*.

I reignited my passion for sport which was my childhood talent. I took up running and ran my first marathon in 1982 where I literally ran myself into the ground. That was the obsessive side of me playing out. I also took up cycling when I had to stop running for eight years because of an injury, and discovered that I was good at that, too. That led me to get into competitive racing, and in the process, came to see that I am competitive in my nature, not always a good think in relationships, but I try to be aware of it.

In 1994, I went to my first Gay Games which were held in New York. These are held every four years and based on the old Olympic model. I won two bronze medals in cycling. To be with 8,000 other lesbians and gays celebrating being ourselves was a deeply felt and exhilarating experience. I was revelling in being with my tribe, especially my sporting tribe. It actually changed the direction of my life

Winning age group Ironman 70.3 World Championship, Florida USA, 2007.

for the next twenty five years that I spent volunteering for the organisation. I went to six games in total. Even though the games that were held in Sydney in 2002 took over my life for six years, it was time spent that I have never regretted, not for a second. I spent three years on the board of the Federation of Gay Games. I had priceless experiences while getting deeply into debt travelling around the world to different meetings. It was really heartening to see how globally connected our LGBTQI family is.

From 1994 to 2018 when the Games were in Paris, there was a paradigm shift (for better or worse), not only in the LGBTQI world, but in the world as a whole. It was marked by the fact that a new generation of young queer folk were benefitting greatly from the previous generation's hard work, and that the time for us to pass the baton and move on had come. So I stepped away.

In the nineties, triathlons had started to become popular and I thought I would try one for my fiftieth birthday. I came third in my age group and I fell in love with the sport that I was wedded to for the next twenty two years. This is where my competitive nature, obsessiveness, and propensity to be disciplined (which I learned in my recovery process) really came together.

For the next twenty-two years, my life was on repeat. It consisted of early mornings, early nights, training, working, eating, sleeping, racing, travelling, and spending a shitload of money on coaching, equipment and travel costs.

I did ten Ironman races. The distances covered in these races are a 3.9 km swim, a 180.2 km bike ride and a 42.2 km run. Two of those were in Kona, Hawaii, which is the holy grail location for the triathlon world. I won several races in the shorter distances, and actually became an Age Group World Champion at a race in Florida. This was made possible by a big credit card debt, but hey, I've never looked back.

Naturally, there were many accidents and injuries along the way. I actually had six surgeries. The most serious of those involved a hip replacement and shoulder surgery after being hit in a cycle race. I've also had countless muscle tears and plenty of angst around not being able to train. This is all par for the course.

But oh, the travel! That was another passion I discovered. Due to the generosity of my 'husband' whose superannuation I inherited, I sold my unit and moved into an affordable 'retirement' village.

Some older people seem to retire from life itself in these villages – not me. The affordability of these arrangements has given me the chance to be out enjoying the sunset years of my life with verve and vitality.

I retired from the world of Triathlon at 69. It was time to get off that treadmill of doing the same old routine – albeit slower and with slightly less verve. There were other challenges to be had. I have spent seven years going around the planet, sometimes in small groups visiting old friends, trekking in Europe, USA, South America (especially Peru, Patagonia and Cuba) and experiencing the wondrous Antarctica. Oh, Antarctica, pretty much the only pristine spot on the planet, although sadly this is changing. It was there that at times I felt deeply and intensely connected to the earth when I looked at the starkly blue icebergs, the breaching whales, enjoying the quietness, and the very funny penguins who just go about their particular mission

Running keeps me sane, 2022.

Member of Planet Ukelele, 2025.

in life. I really felt that we are just such a tiny, unimportant pinprick in the weave of the universe, and that maybe there is something greater than us mere mortals.

It's said that travel is the University of Life. I couldn't agree more. Not being one to be in a comfort zone all the time meant that I was way out of mine many times over. I don't regret any of it. I am still travelling (and cat-sitting), but they tend to be shorter trips and with more time spent in the UK. After all of these years, I've got to appreciate that the UK is my spiritual home. I'm not too keen on the winter though, but spending time with my ever-increasing family has become more important the older I get. I now have three nieces, one nephew, six great-nephews and three great-nieces.

Once the big travel adventures came to an end, it was time for me to find another hobby. I had always wanted to try a new musical instrument after giving the piano away in my teenage years. How about the ukulele, I thought? How hard could it be with only four strings? Famous last words!

I found an amazing ukulele teacher who I now count as a close friend. Lindy Sardelic who is an actor and musician (amongst her many other talents) is also an amazing and patient teacher. After four years of tuition and practice, I have gone from being on L plates to my second year of P plates.

Lindy introduced me to Planet Ukulele. A world full of mostly older types, who meet and play for fun, with the emphasis on the fun. Three chords were what the punk era played, and on a ukulele, that is enough. That said, there are many who play who are true virtuosos.

My ability to be disciplined has kicked in again as I

practice most days. Am I good at it? In my assessment I am competent, but I have probably missed the boat in terms of my fantasy of being a rock star! I have added a fully electric ukulele to my collection, so I get to play around with that as well. There's nothing like learning to play the blues and good old rock and roll.

I continue to run, swim, and cycle, purely for health and enjoyment. My body says I need to keep moving until I can't. I am part of a great running squad, the eldest by many years and yet those in the group are so supportive of me turning up regardless.

Relationships? Given that I never really knew what a healthy relationship was, and didn't understand personal boundaries or how to protect myself, I will never know if the childhood abuse and then the rape robbed me of ever really being intimate and fully trusting another person again.

I am acutely aware that I have never really experienced being with a partner in a committed relationship for a long length of time. Yet in my sunset years, I feel mature enough and emotionally healthy enough to embark on a partnership, but I figure that ship has sailed. I do feel sad about this aspect of my life journey but accept that I can't change the past, only the now.

That said, I have many loving friends some of whom are very close, and feel like I am a good confident and trustworthy friend myself.

But more than anything, for the most part, I finally spend more time with peace of mind than I spend having low days. To me, that is priceless. It may have taken me most of my life to get here, but I cherish this place and don't take it for granted.

# Epilogue

Life is ephemeral, and it can vanish in a puff at any time. I would like to feel that I will leave a handful of stardust rather than dirt and dust behind me by making a tiny contribution to making this mad world a little better.

When I think about why we humans are here and what our mission is or what the purpose of it all is, the only answer I ever come up with is still – How the fuck would I know!

# About the Author

Kate Rowe is a force of nature. For someone whose lived experience would have challenged others who are less tenacious than she is, Kate is writing books, speaking at events, playing her ukulele and running marathons as she moves through her seventh decade.

If you would like to engage Kate to speak at your event, or contact her for any other reason, you can email her at katerowe51@outlook.com

www.ingramcontent.com/pod-product-compliance
Lightning Source LLC
Chambersburg PA
CBHW061732070526
44583CB00024B/3114